Come Alive

Don't Just Exist

Meher Mirchandani

Come Alive
Copyright © 2020 Meher Mirchandani
First published in 2020

ISBN
Paperback: 978-1-922456-16-8
Ebook: 978-1-922456-17-5

All rights reserved. No part of this book may be reproduced, stored in a retrieval system, or transmitted by any means (electronic, mechanical, photocopying, recording, or otherwise) without written permission from the author.

Because of the dynamic nature of the Internet, any web addresses or links contained in this book may have changed since publication and may no longer be valid. The information in this book is based on the author's experiences and opinions. The views expressed in this book are solely those of the author and do not necessarily reflect the views of the publisher; the publisher hereby disclaims any responsibility for them.

The author of this book does not dispense any form of medical, legal, financial, or technical advice either directly or indirectly. The intent of the author is solely to provide information of a general nature to help you in your quest for personal development and growth. In the event you use any of the information in this book, the author and the publisher assume no responsibility for your actions. If any form of expert assistance is required, the services of a competent professional should be sought.

Publishing information
Publishing, design, and production facilitated by Passionpreneur Publishing,
A division of Passionpreneur Organization Pty Ltd, ABN: 48640637529
Book Cover design by Dipti Lahori Nazare (Design 1.618)

www.PassionpreneurPublishing.com
Melbourne, VIC | Australia

Dedication

I dedicate this book to you; holding this book in your hand is a signal and a message that your evolutionary path has begun. Take charge head on, you are limitless!

Everything that you want, you already are.
—*Rumi*

TESTIMONIALS

Entrepreneur, business leader and coach, Meher Mirchandani is indeed a remarkable woman. Professional and hardworking, caring and compassionate she has been able to wisely articulate her business responsibilities with her role as a coach, wife and mother. She leads by example and she is very strongly ethically grounded.

—Malik Sacoor, Chairman, Sacoor Brothers

Meher is a source of positive energy, light, love and happiness. Blessed to have her in my life. Very grateful for her!

—Alisha Moopen, Deputy Managing Director, Aster DM

Meher has provided me and my charity Harmony House an overwhelming amount of support during the past 8 years. Her compassion, empathy, and huge heart allows her to fully connect to all that meet her. It has been wonderful to witness her journey along the path of love, purpose and enlightenment.

— Lucy Bruce, Founder, Harmony House and Co-founder, Home Grown Eco Friendly Nursery

Meher is a very insightful coach and asks pertinent questions. Her coaching style is firm but friendly. Meher helped me make tough business and personal decisions. She is an awesome individual with high energy, integrity, and patience. Meher is full of life and leads life to the fullest. She is a great coach and listener. I would highly recommend Meher to be a high performance coach for people who want to grow and accomplish new heights.

—Juuhi Ahuja, President, Wise Men Consultants

I have worked with Meher now for over 1.5 years in Manrre, our real estate fund, and she is one of the most skilled, efficient, and influential professionals I have ever dealt with. Her best ability is to influence people by coaching and mentoring them to become the best version of themselves. She has contributed to my professional development by constantly coaching me to grow myself by attending learning events and motivating me and our team to get beyond our comfort zone. She is always striving to be the best in people management and has contributed positively to all of us in the team.

—Arpit Juneja, CFO, Palmon Group

Meher has always been a positive person and supportive friend. She has inspired me to shift my energy to focus on myself which has made a huge positive difference in my life. I learnt the power of affirmations and self-healing through her coaching, I am grateful to have her as a friend and my coach.

—Arshiya Merchant, Homemaker

Meher has been instrumental in changing my perception on work life and personal life balance. Her committed devotion and dedication to both her family and work responsibilities *has been a source of motivation and a great example of what women can achieve. Her spiritual journey has enlightened and inspired me to live life positively and full of gratitude.*

—**Namita Hingorani, Homemaker**

Table of Contents

Introduction — xi
Acknowledgements — xv

1 My Journey — 1
2 Love is a Process — 17
3 An Introduction to You — 29
4 Understanding Pain — 41
5 Reprogramming Yourself — 55
6 Serving Your Soul — 67
7 Be in Love — 77
8 Conclusion — 85

Introduction

Knowledge of Self is the ultimate knowledge. The substratum of all Knowledge. Pure Awareness, Consciousness, Knowledge which makes you all-knowing. This concept baffles the human mind. Yet it is true. A simple example illustrates this truth. Consider a person ignorant of directions. Give him one direction. Point out east. Instantly he can fix west, north, and south. Also, northeast and southwest, northwest, and southeast. Thus, he can fix all the possible directions just from one. Similarly, with the Knowledge of Self, you become the knowing-Principle, the basis of all Knowledge.

—*Bhagavad Gita*

YOUR EXPERIENCE ON this earth is meant to be Transcendental, Sublime, and Blissful with you feeling liberated, selfless, and loveful.

Are you living and alive? Are you soaring and free?

It is very common for most of us to spend our whole life waiting to start living.

Come Alive is my mission to release the pain inside you—the pain that I felt for fourteen years of my life. I would like you to gain the courage through my experiences and learning so you can release the pain and feel the beauty, bliss, and magic of life.

I want to you to become aware of your purpose to exercise your truth of being; I want you to feel love in each and every cell of your body and be in love with life and yourself and everything as it is in the now. I want you to be grateful for being who you are, to forgive, and to live in faith.

We have all grown up to believe love is a process that completes us when we love another, and they love us back as per our expectations. This is purely to fulfil our inadequacies we hold. If there is something missing in your life, it is you. There was nothing missing in my life except me. I had everything I could dream of, but I was not accepting and loving myself for who I was, and hence I could not feel the love I was receiving.

Through this book, I am here to challenge this and repaint these images created in our head, to disrupt your belief of inadequacy, and to rebuild a belief of pure love which originates from within. In this book I will share with you my experience of love and the process to fall in love with yourself. Because it all starts with you!

Every day you must jump out of bed as a better version of yourself, charged with the energy of being in love with yourself and your life. If you are unable to feel this, then let's make the shift now so you can start feeling this.

What stands in the way of our love, peace, and happiness is ourself. We hold ourself from our greatness. We need to understand and recognise that we are not our thoughts in our head; we need to change those thoughts and inner voices. We can achieve what we want in life if we work on making ourself the master, and for that we need to be committed to acknowledging ourself by consistently working on ourselves.

Come join me on the journey to transform yourself through a five-phase process that will help you to know and prioritise yourself!

*If you want the best the world has to offer,
offer the world your best.*

—*Neale Donald Walsch*

Acknowledgements

I am grateful to

My Spiritual Master
SSDN

My parents, Manohar and Reshma Lahori, for the love and the life they have given me. I am what I am because they have been beside me unconditionally.

My in-laws, Moolchand Khemchand and Bindu Khemchand, for the support throughout my journey.

My husband, Anand Mirchandani, for evolving with me.

My daughters, Vaaniya and Vihana Mirchandani, for bringing divine love into my life.

My siblings, Kunal Lahori and Dipti Lahori-Nazare, for believing in me.

My mentor, Juuhi Ahuja, for guiding me and encouraging me to do my best and be my best.

My friends, Yogesh Sajnani and Riddhima Whabi, for their love, time, and attention when I most needed it.

My team at the Palmon Group for standing with me and appreciating me.

My EO Forum members and EO for providing a perspective which is needed to progress in life.

Everyone who has come along on my journey, as they have helped me become who I am meant to be!

Credits and Gratitude to the teachers whose learning have made me who I am meant to be.

Joe Dispenza
Bruce Lipton
Dandapani
Peter Crone
Eckhart Tolle
Mo Gawdat
Gary Zukav
Hal Elrod
Rhonda Byrne
Oprah Winfrey
Neal Donald Walsch
Brian Rose
Rumi

1
My Journey
From Victim to Victor

All problems are illusions of the mind.

—*Eckhart Tolle*

IN THE YEAR 1981, I was born to the most amazing, loving, and caring couple I have ever known. From the day I was brought on to the earth by my parents, all I have received from them is unconditional love. They showered me with the best of everything life has to offer even before I requested.

Growing up, I travelled the world with my parents—from Vegas to Hong Kong—in Concordes and cruises. The first car I drove was an S-class, and I was chauffeured to school in a Rolls-Royce.

Our summers included trips to New York and Europe, where we spent beautiful days as a family—sightseeing, shopping, and enjoying the luxuries of life.

My mom—along with being perfect—follows a spiritual master and is extremely spiritual, which always gave depth to her life. For her, life was a perfect balance of spiritualism and luxuries, which flowed into our lives too.

All through my childhood, I was showered with immense love. I am my parents' most treasured gem, and I felt it all through my growing years. They have always been with me at every stage of my life, making me feel that I am the most important person in their life.

What else could I have wanted to feel loved and complete? What else could I ask for? Was this not the love everyone is looking for? There was not a thing missing in my life.

However, something was amiss! I received love like none other, but I didn't feel any of it. I was born in the riches of this world, but love was a far-fetched feeling.

In the winter of 2003, I was married to the man I loved. It was the first wedding in the family, and it was a big fat Indian one. The celebrations spanned over a week, with family and friends flown in from all over the world. The themed ceremonies were conducted in the best locations of Dubai including the Burj-Al-Arab. A dream wedding had come true for me, which remains a dream for many. My parents did everything in their capacity to make my wedding beyond what I had dreamt of. My in-laws are the sweetest, most supportive, and most loving people on this planet. They adorned me with everything I had wanted.

Love holds a very special and important part in my life, and the expression of it is equally important to me. While marriages are made in heaven, in the Hindu scriptures, marriages are also considered to be a holy union of two souls forever. Marriage is more than a physical union; it is a spiritual and emotional union. This union mirrors the one between God and His Church. It is an extremely sacred bond that lasts a lifetime.

My husband, Anand, and I had a short but sweet courtship and a perfect few months, and then the reality hit. It was nothing like I had imagined. Marriage was nothing like it was meant to be. It seemed like we got married too young. We didn't have the time to know ourselves, let alone knowing one another. I got married within eighteen months of graduating from university. The transition from being a child to being married and living as a couple with the in-laws and serving them was too huge for me to handle. At twenty-two, I was at the peak of my life—full of love, enthusiasm, and excitement. I was not ready to take any responsibility.

All these expectations shattered me. Was this the day I was waiting for to feel the love that will complete me? I was full of energy waiting to live life in its most vibrant form. But Anand's definition of love and life was different from mine. For him, love and life were about his service to his parents, family, and his spiritual master, which I respect today, but at twenty-two, I was not ready for that. All I wanted to feel then was the love of a companion, a lover, and a husband.

We had a courtship period of two years, which was not enough to know or experience anything with the person you want to spend the rest of your life with. Further, there was a firm belief in our culture that friendship and love in a relationship starts after the wedding and hence I believed that we would be spending time together. But, men usually have different programming and outlook of the world than that of women. The challenges for a man are different as he needs to now take up the role of being a breadwinner for the family and carve a path to success. So, Anand was focussed on making life better for us together. In the midst of all this, it is challenging for the young couple to spend time and value each other. In most Indian families up until a few years ago, the son stays home with his parents, and hence, they say a marriage is not between two individuals but between two families. This was also the case with me.

Before I got married, I had started my fashion brand Meher & Riddhima and had a vision for it. But after I got married, it was extremely challenging for me to work as my expected first priority was to take care of the household with my mother-in-law. Though my mother-in-law has been my biggest supporter, my inexperience and lack of knowledge of myself, along with the short courtship with Anand, made me suffer in my head.

While the families were on good terms with each other, they did a business transaction, which went bitter after a few years when the recession hit in 2008. I did my best to involve myself and help solve the situation, but nothing worked.

The conflict between my father and my husband was the most challenging and devastating part of my journey. The pain paralyzed me in every way. I couldn't feel anything—no joy, no pain; nothing excited me. I was so dead inside. The rosy picture that I had painted based on my beliefs of a loving life had come to an end.

I couldn't live. I needed so much help. I didn't know why all the circumstances were against me. I felt like a victim that was hit from all the areas in my life. I didn't know how to solve the situation. I didn't have the strength or the vision to get out of the dark tunnel I was in. I didn't know what life was about. I had questions on my existence.

I asked myself things like

- I have had such a blessed and privileged life, but what did I do wrong?
- Is my life like this because I chose the wrong partner?
- I couldn't remember hurting anyone in my life, so why was I being hurt and in so much pain?
- What karma am I paying for?
- What am I doing in this life? Why am I here on this planet?

All I remember is that my heart was crying every single minute of the day. It was extremely hurtful to see my father and my husband in conflict, and while Anand was doing his best to navigate the issue, it was difficult to rise from it. Anand was disgruntled with himself for partnering with my father, which led to a wedge between us. I started fearing my husband even before we started loving each other. I lived in the hope of being born in a new life as a new person and have new experiences. I didn't want to cause any karma that would give me a harder life next time around. So, I lived my life silently.

Escaping the Pain
Every situation after my marriage challenged me to go within, but I was not aware, and I couldn't see the signs. I was confused and perplexed at my meaning of love. A marriage, for me, stood for selfless service and unconditional love, but I didn't feel any love at all. I couldn't receive anything. My beliefs of expectations, attachment, love, and so many other things were not aligned with my life. My programming was not serving me.

In 2009, with a friend's guidance, I started learning Theta Healing. It really helped me, and soon, I completed eight levels of Theta Healing, became a healer, and then, after a few years, became a teacher. I started to look within to heal myself and my relationship. This path started my evolution. However, I still didn't figure out what was I missing and not seeing. I kept searching for love and happiness because I just didn't feel it in anything I did and from anyone. I was just not receiving it even after my healings and learning.

To numb the pain, I started focusing on my brand. With time, I could see progress in it. Meher & Riddhima was at twenty-five stores across the GCC and the US. It was worn by celebrities and had won several awards and nominations over the last fifteen years. I received success at work, I had fame and recognition, but I didn't feel content.

Each time I would think, "Once I achieve a certain milestone, I will feel happy and fulfilled." I kept making plans for business and worked on expansion. I reached a million dollars in turnover and entered the US market. It was my dream to be a designer supplying in the US alongside my favourite designers like Donna Karan and others. I believed happiness was a destination, but it was only later that I realised it is a journey. And life was soon filled with tasks and things that I did as an escape mechanism. When you are busy with things to do and things to buy, it is a drug to numb your pain.

After a long wait, in 2012, I was blessed with the wonderful gift of being a mother and given twice the love, with two beautiful angels and a new meaning to life. It was by far the most beautiful feeling and most love-showering experience. I was super happy and grateful.

While I felt the blessing of the divine, I also had a feeling that life was over at thirty-one. I had such challenging nine years, and now these angels were my purpose and reason to live and whatever else I wanted to do in life would have to be done in my next life. This was a huge responsibility given to me by God, and I had to honour it.

Due to the dispute between our families, my parents were not present at my delivery and in the hospital. Every woman wants her mother by her side at her delivery, and today, I know that a mother wants the same. But I didn't have that privilege, and it was my first delivery with my twins. All I wanted was my mother to be by my side. Though my husband and his parents were there with me throughout the process with all the love, I couldn't feel any of it. Fear, anxiety, and pain had crippled my mind, body, and soul. I had reached rock bottom.

After the twins were born, there was a huge shift in Anand, and it definitely evolved our relationship. The twins brought a new energy into our lives and our home was filled with love, happiness, and excitement. Anand is the best father ever; the twins are his topmost priority, and the love, attention, and time he gives them is beyond expression. I am grateful for him being the father he is.

As for me, all desires were extinguished; there was no reason to live except my daughters.

I felt I was wasting life but didn't know what I was supposed to be doing. I was living in the dark and couldn't see any light. While all along I was receiving messages, I was unable to understand them.

> So, I waited...
> I waited with gratitude,
> I waited with unconditional love,
> I waited with selfless service, and
> I waited with all the love in my heart.

In September 2015, I joined my family business as the managing director of the group and joined the Entrepreneurs' Organization (EO). EO gave me great insights to life and business, and with the help of my forum I was able to evolve myself, my life, and my relationship.

I was soon on the *Forbes* list of Next Generation Entrepreneurs in the UAE and other such lists. I was meeting peers from different walks of life. Knowing their perspectives and experiences added immense value to me and life became a little easier.

However, I still felt I was missing something—something I was unable to see and understand; something was incomplete inside me.

Though I became mindful and driven to learn more about the life beyond, it still felt like I was walking in the dark.

Bestowed with Messages
In August 2017, my conversations with friends became meaningful for my growth, which I heard as messages. When I would speak to friends, it seemed they were answering the questions I had in my life. At times, it felt that they were leading me to some place I was meant to be going. I heard experiences of people that hit me and pushed me to start making changes in my life. I started believing I could live a rewarding life with a few shifts in my life. A series of incidents, reflections, and learnings drove me to past life regression therapy. When I experienced my past lives, I realised the value of my current life. My past life gave me the perception, awareness, and learning that I had wasted a lifetime seeking for love from another and it was now time to find the true meaning of love and my purpose in this life.

The start of my transformation was from a book called *The Miracle Morning* by Hal Elrod, which gave me the power that I needed to start living by and taking care of myself.

- Exercise, meditation, journal, gratitude, forgiveness—this became my daily routine.
- I went on a forgiveness journey, started journaling every day about everyone I needed to forgive, and made sure that, most importantly, I need to keep forgiving myself.
- I started a gratitude journey, where I saw the blessing in everything that has happened with me and thanked myself, everyone involved, and the universe.
- I meditated and journaled about how to transform lower-energy feelings to higher-energy ones.
- I read every day—from someone who didn't enjoy reading, I went on to read almost twenty-five books in twenty-four months on different theories, biographies, self-growth, and business.
- I started exercising regularly as I believed that our body is a temple in which we have to live for this entire life.
- I started working and succeeding from within, and that's when the transformation began.

Taking care of myself in every aspect of my life was the start of my love story with myself.

Experiencing the Magic
On consistently following my daily routine, I started receiving answers to what I was seeking in meditation sessions. My fear started transforming into courage and my anxiety into faith. I started working deeply on myself to remove all the negative feelings from past life and this life. On building my connection with my soul and connecting daily with

my higher self, I felt so much love. It was exactly like I had wanted to feel.

I was finally fulfilled, fulfilled to the core. It was only when I connected with myself, I knew who I was. It was only when I loved myself that I knew what love was. It was only when I served myself, I knew what service to humanity was!

In a year of focussed practice, I had transformed into a new being, I was alive. I was so alive that I could feel life in each and every cell of my body. I didn't even realise how dead I was until I came alive. My transformation felt like a miracle; I didn't know it was possible to transform and live a new life that you desired in the same life because I had written my life off. I didn't think it would happen. This was what magic felt like!

Rising Myself
Now that I had learned the magic, I could not keep it to myself. I had to share it with the world, so I started acquiring and practising the tools to contribute. Having done Theta Healing, Basic DNA, Advance DNA, DNA 3, Manifestation, Intuitive Anatomy; and Basic, Advance, and Intuitive Instructors; and Dig Deeper, I could now heal myself even more since I had discovered the root belief. I started to help people the same way I helped myself.

In 2018, I launched the Palmon Foundation with my mother as a CSR Initiative for our organisation. Palmon Foundation provides students in India, Nepal, and Bangladesh who aspire to study further than the tenth grade, with scholarships to pursue higher studies. They are selected carefully with a formal interview and made to commit to their selected education field and term. Scholarship is granted based on the determination and ability to fulfil their promise of being disciplined and achieving their best. Students are often from families that are below the poverty line. They are vetted and mentored throughout their higher education for emotional strength and to remain motivated.

In 2019, I embarked on a journey of coaching and became a Transformative Co-Active Professional coach from the Coaches Training Institute (CTI), which is one of the largest and most established professional coach training organisation in the world. Co-Active Coaching greatly adds perception and empowers us on a journey of opening consciousness. It gave me the tools to effectively communicate and serve the world with knowledge.

As an entrepreneur, your team is the first touchpoint of people you can motivate to live better, and I do that with 100 percent dedication. Then it is the lives of friends and family that you can inspire, which has been truly rewarding. And now I move into the world with my mission, when your purpose is to create the same magic that has been created in your life, the universe supports you, and I am blessed and grateful to feel the support.

Thank you for allowing me the opportunity to introspect and evolve on this journey called life—not possible without you.

—Sumeet Shewakramani,
Managing Director, DBMSC Steel

I have always believed that everyone comes into our lives for a reason. I have known Meher for the last sixteen years and we instantly connected.

Beyond that, two years back when I lost my beloved mother, my life had almost come to a standstill. Meher, at that point of my life, made a significant impact in my journey. She introduced me to a book Many Lives, Many Masters, *which had some answers to my unfathomable questions. She then gifted me* The Miracle Morning *with a special handwritten note. Her thoughtful words and questions were a catalyst for me to overcome my limited belief that I am not "quite a reader."*

Moving forward, Meher has positively influenced my inner self and strength with all the books that she maps out for me to read and with all the insightful conversations we have had for hours.

Thank you, Meher, for being a part of my journey and in my circle of influence—You are simply one of the nicest, most genuine and inspiring person.

I look forward to many more meaningful moments with you.

—Heerral Asnani, Admin, Clarion School

I feel extremely grateful to have guided Heerral to rise from her pain, and I believe we experience pain for the light to enter, and this was the case with her too. Her transformation is impressive and her expression of my contribution to her life is my reason of being.

My mission now became to evoke the same transformation in as many people as I could; this is my purpose and my reason to incarnate. And this led me to further invest in myself and learn the tools, information, and knowledge to contribute to fellow humans so they can experience this beautiful life in all its glory. I then perused neuro-linguistic programming (NLP) and became an NLP practitioner.

I soon started contributing my time to heal and coach fellow humans who were aspiring to know and honour themselves through the five-phase process so they could connect to their inner being, fall in love with themselves, and come alive!

My journey taught me that the purpose of awakenings is to be aware of certain truths, love, and your true existence as a soul. To trigger such awakening, we need to be tough in challenging situations. If the situation in our life is favourable to what we want, there will be no awakening. We go through emotional turmoil and feel the deepest pain, fear, rejection, abandonment, guilt, doubt, and a lot more because we have to work on these issues inside us and only then true awakening happens. The new us takes birth!

As soon as the new me took birth, my life evolved to a higher level. The path of challenge became grace, and this happens when we become aware that every circumstance and event in life is for our highest and best. Come, join me as I unfold my love story in my first book *Come Alive* and contribute to my mission of evoking the transformation in you so you are able to celebrate yourself every single moment.

Brace yourself!

Know what sparks the light in you. Then use the light to illuminate the world.

—*Oprah Winfrey*

2
Love is a Process
It Starts with You

Our deepest fear is not that we are inadequate. Our deepest fear is that we are powerful beyond measure. It is our light, not our darkness that most frightens us. We ask ourselves, "Who am I to be brilliant, gorgeous, talented, and fabulous?" Actually, who are you not to be?

—Marianne Williamson

ARE YOU READY to join my journey to complete you? Together we will discover that there is nothing missing in life and that we are enough! And the day we are aware of this truth, our potential of being unlimited and creating the life we want will be in our hands.

This chapter will unfold a new perspective to love. It will help you realise love is a process of going within to emerge as a lover of yourself. Love is not something you do; it is a way of being. It has nothing to do with anyone else. It's all about us. When you get love into your being by accepting, appreciating, and acknowledging yourself for who you are, you open the receptors to feel love in each and every cell of your body. When you are in love with yourself, the universe is in love with you. And you will feel it!

What stands in the way of our love, peace, and happiness is our self. We hold our self from our greatness. We need to understand and recognise that the thought in our head is not who we are. You are ready to grow when you realise that the "I" who is always talking inside your head is determining your state of being, and you need to differentiate the thought from yourself. We need to change those thoughts and inner voices, or silence them. We can achieve what we want in life if we work on making our self the master, and that needs us to be committed to ourself.

This chapter is meant to shake the beliefs we hold, from the Disney tales/movies that we have watched growing up, to the stories and the books we have read; all teach us that the love of another will fulfil us and complete us. I am here to challenge this and repaint these images created in our head, disrupt your belief of inadequacy, and rebuild a belief of pure love, which originates from within. In this book, I will share with you my experience of love and the process to fall in love with yourself—because it starts with you!

We have all grown up to believe love is a process that completes us when we love another, and they love us back as per our expectations. This is purely to fulfil our inadequacies we hold for ourselves. If there is something missing in your life, it is you. There was nothing missing in my life except me. As mentioned in the previous chapter I had everything I could dream of, but I did not accept and love myself for who I was, and hence I could not feel the love I was receiving.

Drawing reference from Peter Crone, I believe the feeling of inadequacy, which is inherent in most humans, is an illusion; what we are not is an obstacle to experiencing what we are. "I am not loved" is an aspect of the persona; it is not the truth, it is an illusion. Our programming and belief system make us feel this. My past life experience was so strong that even after having everything in my current life, I felt incomplete. The illusion that I am not enough emerges from our programming in childhood and even goes back to our past lives at times.

Once we understand that the programme that we live in is a direct relation to how we are, we create the awareness to start the work. To explain this further, I have seen that in most cases the life that a woman leads inherently is very similar to what her mother has led. It is because the mother receives the programmes from her mother and then passes them on unconsciously to her daughter.

An experience I would like to share: I had a client who always feared that her daughter would be married to a man whose mother will be in conflict with her, because the client had experienced this all her life. Going back to her past in the session, we discovered that her mother too had a mother-in-law who made her life a living hell. The programming can be passed on generation to generation, like genes. The truth is beliefs are unconsciously passed on, and when you choose to understand and accept it, then you can work to break the chain.

The awareness that something is missing comes from the soul and must be addressed as soon as you feel it. Most of the times we don't know, and we live to fulfil our personality keeping the message of our soul unheard.

I ignored my soul for most of my life. When I was in the fashion business and started my business in 2002, all I wanted was to succeed and have my clothes worn by celebrities, stocked at top stores of the world, and showcasing at New York fashion week. I didn't do anything beyond this. I believed once I reached this destination, I will be the happiest person on this earth. The transitory relief was believed to be the solution to my issues I was facing internally. The metaphor I like to give is of a painkiller—when we are in pain in our hearts and soul, we aim to achieve momentary happiness and peace by indulging in addictions: work, money, possessions, rigorous training, alcohol, coffee, smoking, etc. Everyone gets a temporary high on different things, and they become our painkillers to move forward in life seeming happy. The addictions are often camouflaged as stress relievers as the brain registers all pleasures in the same way, whether they originate with a psychoactive drug, a monetary reward, a sexual encounter, or a satisfying meal. In the brain, pleasure has a distinct signature: the release of the neurotransmitter dopamine in the nucleus accumbens.

Inviting a reflection for a moment, life is mostly viewed as a series of achievements and growth in status. What we see, appreciate, and speak about most of the time are the achievements of the personality—financial growth, awards, accolades, and material success of people. We are drawn to the network of people we know.

How often do we stop and ask anyone or Google the relationship they have with themselves? How often do we think beyond the financial and materialistic growth we work for every single day? When is the development of a human being the news headlines? We all know about the drops and picks in the markets every day. We talk more about Warren Buffett and Bill Gates than Joe Dispenza and Sadhguru. All our collective energies are focussed on the material growth of the personality, but let me tell you there is not enough of anything in the world to mitigate your belief of not being enough and incomplete.

Being in the fashion business for fifteen years, I followed the fashion industry closely, and I was always shocked to discover how super successful people take to suicide, earning everything that anyone would ever want. I studied about the famous Alexander McQueen in fashion school and was saddened to discover that he overdosed to death.

His work is an inspiration to the world; the designer was honoured as Commander of the Most Excellent Order of the

British Empire by Queen Elizabeth II in 2003, and won numerous other awards in the fashion world. His achievements in fashion earned him the British Designer of the Year awards four times (1996, 1997, 2001, and 2003), as well as the CFDA's International Designer of the Year award in 2003.

A son of a taxi driver, McQueen founded his own Alexander McQueen label in 1992 and worked at Givenchy from 1996-2001. At the age of forty in 2010, he lived in Mayfair and was personally worth 30 million dollars. From Lady Gaga to Prince Charles everyone adored, admired, and wore his designs.

To name a few other famous personalities, Marilyn Monroe had everything that a person could want: fame, beauty, and money. However, underneath her bombshell looks, Monroe faced many demons that ultimately led to her death. If she was complete, would she have committed suicide?

Kate Spade is another recent death in fashion; her brand was worth 2.4 billion dollars and sold to Coach. She and her husband built the Kate Spade brand from the ground up with no experience in retail design or production. The couple had to learn everything themselves, using their apartment as an office, design studio, and home. She left a legacy that anyone would want to leave. If she had felt she was enough, would she want to take her own life? If she was fulfilled and complete, would she not want to live on to experience this beautiful life?

All of us look for love and happiness in the wrong places like status, pleasure, addiction, and more. No one looks for it in the right place. And I did too, as these are the beliefs created while in school and university. All we were taught is that our materialistic achievements are considered as success in this world. What about our persona and spiritual growth, why are there no metrics on those? Have you ever thought about it? Why are we not forced to take soul studies like Math and English?

If we were taught to take care of our soul in school, we would be powerful and loving beings. Vibrating at a different frequency and along with working on our financial success, we would be abundantly peaceful and happy.

I was listed on the *Forbes* Next Gen, won awards, accolades, and nominations but still did not feel complete. I was working in a job I always dreamt of but didn't feel alive. That's when you know there is something deeper to conquer in life.

The feeling that something was missing didn't stop until I finally met me, fell in love with myself, and came alive. The realisation came from a series of incidents, reflections, and learnings. The love that I am looking for in the world is inside me; the love that I am expecting from another is what I should be expecting from myself. This was the awareness that came along with the understanding that I am not seated on the seat of my soul and hence I am feeling incomplete. Once I started working on all of these aspects, I gained authentic power and fulfilment in all areas of my life. My love for life, myself, my journey, and my evolution emerged.

To fall in love with yourself, you have to know yourself, nurture yourself, and appreciate yourself. It is a process to go within, and only then you can emerge as a lover of yourself.

My mission is to evoke the transformation in you so you are able to celebrate yourself every single moment. Through this book I am committed to start the process in you. I have divided the process into five phases. They are mentioned below.

1. Knowing yourself
Why is it important to know yourself? We will answer this most important question in the next chapter. And once you understand why it is important to know yourself, we will transition into who I am? What do I like? What fulfils me? What makes me alive? When am I living my best version? I will introduce you to you!

2. Identifying who I am
Beliefs create feelings. Beliefs are created based on our experiences or the experiences and comments of family members either in our growing years or even earlier. And since the subconscious mind is absorbing and open till age seven, they straight go to the subconscious mind. And as we know the subconscious mind is about 95 percent of our brain. In this step, we will go deeper to understand how beliefs are created and how can we identify the programmes related to those beliefs. We will address questions like, what do I feel most of the time? Why do I feel the way I feel? What are the negative feelings in me? What makes me feel sad?

3. Dissolving the beliefs
To overcome and change beliefs is the major part of the process. Once feelings and beliefs (our programming) have been identified, we need to start working on them from the inside. We need guidance, coaching, healing, discipline, and routine (meditation, reading, journaling, gratitude, affirmations, and exercise) to start overcoming them. It is an inside job and needs your commitment.

4. Letting go
Once the above three processes are clear and followed, there will be a lot of things that you will need to let go of. Through tools we can start letting go of all the things that don't serve us, which will include things, people, activities, and thoughts. Your utmost responsibility is to serve yourself, and hence everything else can be allowed to let go.

5. Being in love
Once you have let go, you will feel peace. And here I will express how it feels to be in love with yourself through accepting, appreciating, and nurturing ourselves. When we start living and serving from within with intention and consciously, we start to grow into becoming our best version and falling in love with ourselves for who we are. Our unlimited power emerges, the universe supports us, and we feel it!

We will be able to grow ourselves only when we know ourselves.

—Meher

Nothing will shift unless we don't shift!

Transformational change occurs when we shift limiting beliefs, change our perspective, and live in alignment with our soul.

What we have learned in this chapter is that success doesn't give joy, fame doesn't give peace, and money can't buy bliss!

What stands in the way of eternal happiness is the love we hold for ourselves due to the programming we have that is instilled in our growing up years from external influences. The incorrect belief of inadequacy keeps us away from greatness, peace, and happiness.

We can dissolve this belief through a commitment to the five-phase process, which is a process to rediscover yourself and the power you hold within. The awareness that nothing is missing will come to light through the process. As asked when Michelangelo created David, he mentioned, "David was always there, I just chipped away what was not David." Similarly, all we have to do is to chip away what we are not, to recognise what we are, to experience Love, and to be Alive.

Let's start the process. I am grateful you are with me.

Love after Love

The time will come when, with elation, you will greet yourself arriving at your own door, in your own mirror, and each will smile at the other's welcome, and say, sit here. Eat. You will love again the stranger who was yourself. Give wine. Give bread. Give back your heart to itself, to the stranger who has loved you all your life, whom you ignored for another, who knows you by heart. Take down the love letters from the bookshelf, the photographs, the desperate notes, peel your own image from the mirror. Sit. Feast on your life.

—Derek Walcott

3
An Introduction to You
Knowing Yourself

The purpose of this life and all its experiences is not to make ourselves what we think we should be. It is to unfold who we already are.

—*Gary Zukav*

WHO WE ALREADY are comes to light when we choose consciously; choices affect our evolutionary process, and when we choose consciously, we evolve consciously.

I want you to carefully read this and reflect because there may be a great disparity between who we think we are and who we actually are. This seems a bit odd when you read or hear it; however, most people don't know who they are and end up living in conflict. We often become who we think we should be based on our beliefs and programming.

In this chapter you will learn to uncover yourself and the importance of knowing yourself and how to do it.

Why is it important to know ourselves?

Can you imagine living with someone you don't know? Imagine being with a companion you don't know and have no inclination to do so. How would that feel? Walking life with a stranger with no idea what's inside his/her mind, heart, and soul.

That's exactly how I felt for thirty-six years of my life, and the below story will explain why.

My parents are driven and super successful human beings, so to aim for success was programmed in me way before I knew what life was. When we moved to Dubai, it was the time my father was growing his business multifold. I saw less of him at home, but I felt my life becoming privileged by the years. Every few years we moved into a bigger house and bought a few new cars. And not any car—it was either a Rolls-Royce or a Mercedes. I am not sure I knew if there were other cars that existed in the world.

So, for me to be super ambitious and aim for success was an auto programming as my parents have been extremely successful. I remember my dad has never fallen sick or never taken a day off. He would arrive in the morning from his business trips and head straight to work. His beliefs that "work is worship" and "life is not to be wasted" are something I remember very vividly. And guess who has the same beliefs? Me.

From the time I entered university till I graduated and to the time I launched my brand, I didn't take any breaks. I was laser-focussed on my plan to be successful and famous like him. I graduated in summer of 2002 and launched my brand in September 2002. This was my interpretation of "work is worship" and "life is not to be wasted."

Was this me? I am not sure. I didn't know who I was because I didn't know I could be something else. I didn't invest any time to know who I was, and in fact, being in the fashion business, I was actually in conflict with my soul. Though I love to dress well and love fashion, the business of fashion is dependent on two elements—business and marketing. Though all businesses have the marketing element in it, fashion heavily depends on marketing, which includes extensive socialising—wining and dining and partying. Neither I nor my partners enjoyed this part of the business because my partners are my best friends and we are all introverts; we are vegetarians, and we don't drink. Hence, though our quality, designs, and every other element was perfect the brand perception in the market lagged behind because we were unable to fulfil the rules of the game.

While we were doing our best to be fashion personalities, our soul and personality was not aligned. It's only when the personality comes fully to serve the energy of the soul that its authentic power emerges. And this took me fifteen years to understand because I didn't know me. I struggled to be the person I was not.

So are you aware of who you are?

Do you know what you love to do and why do you love to do it? Are you able to stand up for who you are from an authentic perspective?

What is your authentic self? And how do we discover it?

We build relationships with people by starting to know them and spending time with them; the more time we spend with them, the stronger our relationships get and we also build friendships for life. So this brings us to the question, how strong is our relationship with ourself? What are we doing to spend time with ourselves and know ourselves?

When we are attracted to someone, we love to know about them, their likes, preferences, values, what brings them joy and happiness. What are their hobbies, how do they spend time, what movies they watch? We discuss everything with them in order to integrate and enjoy life with them. In many cases we accept them fully and wish to be accepted fully before committing to be with them for a lifetime.

How do we know ourselves in relation to this? I knew everything about my husband a few years into our marriage. I knew more about him than I knew about me. How often we do something like that? Almost always. It's been only three years since I have known myself. And it's been sixteen years that I have known my husband.

I met myself thirty-eight years ago, but never thought of knowing myself as deep as I wanted to know my husband. Because my programming created the belief that my husband is the most important person in my life and to take care of him through love and appreciation is my utmost responsibility. Because that is the relationship I saw growing up. I saw my mother serving and living for her husband and her children; hence I was programmed in the same way. My mom is a speech therapist by education, and she wanted to practise her profession; however, when she got married my granddad stopped her, and then when she moved to Dubai. She already had two kids who were her top priority. My father needed the support to grow his business, so what she wanted was not important.

When I got married, my husband was my priority, and hence the pattern of my mom was repeated through me. No one teaches us to know ourselves—our soul self— how to nurture ourselves, appreciate ourselves, and be in love with ourselves. We are not our priority. I did and do exactly how my mom did things, which is beautiful, and I am grateful, but it didn't teach me to look at me and honour myself.

Then we were not aware; today we are aware. Hence, similar to the way we spend time with people to know our family and friends and connect to them, we also need to go through the same process to know ourselves. It's exactly the same process as your courtship with another; the only difference is it's with yourself and has to be forever. You must be your priority.

In the words of Louise Hay, "Loving yourself is a wonderful adventure; it's like learning to fly. Imagine if we all had the power to fly at will?" It's a process. To reverse or alter the programming is a process; we need to be patient and loving.

I invite you to start this process with phase one, which is knowing yourself. There are many ways to know yourself. I follow the below to spend time with myself every single day. My life changed the day I read the book, *The Miracle Morning*, by Hal Elrod as it started the process of getting me closer to myself.

1. **Silence and Meditation.** Meditation is a means to move beyond your analytic mind, so you can access your subconscious mind as that's where the magic begins. When we sit in silence, we reason out our thoughts and feelings and dig deep to release them. Most of the time it happens on its own. Meditation empowers you to become more you. It also helps you to silence the voice in your head that is not us. It helps us differentiate our self from the inner chatter (thoughts) that goes on in our head.

2. **Journaling and Gratitude.** Gratitude is the highest form of receivership; when in gratitude, our energy changes, and that's the energy we need to attract the more of what we are in gratitude for. When we journal gratitude or forgiveness, it helps reflections, provides an emotional outlet, helps reduce stress, and shifts our energy. It puts us in an elevated state of being.

3. **Affirmations.** Affirmations are a start to reprogramme the subconscious mind to encourage us to believe certain things about ourselves. They are positive things we say to ourselves or about the world and our place within it. The important thing about affirmations is that it works best once we do it in combination with

other things, and it's something we need to practise daily.

4. **Reading and Learning.** When we commit ourselves to learn new information every single day, we biologically wire that information to our cerebral architecture. And this new information helps us view life, circumstances, and feelings from a new perspective. When we have new perspectives, we make informed choices of our thoughts and actions. It also helps us react better. "The quality of our life, fulfilment and success is not dependent on our circumstances but how we respond to them."—Miles Hilton Barber. Learning is for the mind what air is for your body.

5. **Exercise.** Exercise stimulates the body to release proteins and other chemicals that improve the structure and function of our brain. Exercise helps maintain our health, so we remain fit. It helps with mental fitness, and we are able to focus on all the above things. It also provides us with renewed and increased energy to manage our day with more power. It increases our strength to deal with all fronts of life with elevated energy.

It's not only about making that connection with yourself but also about maintaining it. Like you take a shower every day, you need to shower your mind with your values and your affirmations and your meditations and your love. You need to meet yourself every single day to maintain the relationship you want to build. Practice helps reprogramme your subconscious.

HAL ELROD
THE MIRACLE MORNING
Challenge

SET YOUR ALARM CLOCK 1 HOUR EARLIER

SPEND THIS TIME ON SELF-DEVELOPMENT

PRACTICE THE MIRACLE MORNING LIFE S.A.V.E.R.S

DIVIDE YOUR 60 MINUTES HOWEVER YOU PLEASE

BENEFIT THE REST OF THE DAY FROM YOUR MIRACLE MORNING

#1 SILENCE
Time for reflection, meditation, deep breathing or praying

#2 AFFIRMATION
Room to develop and repeat your positive affirmations

#3 VISUALIZATION
A moment to visualize your goals (possibly with a vision board)

#4 EXERCISE
Benefit mentally from physical exercise with a brief workout

#5 READING
Develop your mind by reading a few pages from a self-help book

#6 SCRIBING
Write down your thoughts by keeping and reviewing a journal

WWW.WANTFORWELLNESS.COM

Your definition of life depends on you; your definition of love depends on you. Was I happy by only serving my personality and its responsibilities? No, I was miserable. I was dying inside every day. I didn't know what was wrong because there was nothing wrong from another's perspective. You have to know yourself and what you want in life to be peaceful.

If you don't know who you are, then you will always live in either assumptions or conflict. There will always be a lack in life, like something is missing. The choice is yours. You want to be aligned to your soul and live a limitlessly powerful life or serve the needs of your personality and waste a lifetime.

Love for me is meeting the person I love the most every single day; hence I schedule the first meeting with myself, where I practise the miracle morning ritual.

The more time you spend with yourself—knowing yourself and working on yourself to be the best version every single day—the more in love you are with yourself.

To be in love with yourself, the first step is to know yourself; you can't be in love with someone you don't know. It just doesn't work.

To know yourself, it is imperative to spend time with yourself. You will never know yourself or another if you don't spend time with them. So, start spending time.

Most importantly, you have to maintain the connection and relationship with yourself; hence, you have to meet yourself every single day to shower yourself with all the love and understanding. In the words of Jane Travis, the relationship with yourself sets the tone of every other relationship you have. Hence it is imperative to know who we are and be in a loving relationship with ourself.

As we approach the end of this chapter, I would like you to spend a little extra time with yourself this week and notice the difference. Spending sixty minutes a day doing different things with yourself will add immense value to you and your life and your relationships. By starting to get responsible for yourself, your mind, your soul, and your body you will connect to yourself. And once you connect to yourself you will begin to discover the authentic power that is within you. This is your first step towards aligning your soul with your personality.

When we align our soul with our personality, we discover our true self, and to be able to discover ourselves, we need to embrace the process to go within and spend time with ourselves.

Once we commit to spending time with ourselves, the journey has begun. In the next chapter, we will start knowing ourselves deeper—that is, identifying the feelings inside us, or what are we feeling most of the time. We will try to understand pain. Why are we feeling what we are feeling? What are the programmes and limiting beliefs we are holding that is keeping us away from greatness and causing our body and heart to be in pain?

Nothing is worth it without purpose and direction, and how can we be guided to our purpose if we don't know who we are?

—*Meher*

4
Understanding Pain
Identifying Limiting Beliefs Causing Pain

Anything that you resent and strongly react to in another is also in you.

—Eckhart Tolle

LIFE IS NOT meant to make you happy; it is meant to challenge you. If there is no challenge in your life, there will be no evolution and awakening. Every moment in life is in line with your growth, and to awaken to this truth is to start living your purpose.

It is very common for people to spend their whole life waiting to start living. Are you living and alive? Are you soaring and free?

Most people live in some sort of pain and more—pain of not being loved, pain of not being appreciated, pain of not being heard, and it continues.

We all have illusions of pain inside us caused by expectations from another or the universe. What we fail to understand is that this is an illusion and is self-inflicted. To be able to set ourself free, we need to carefully identify the feelings of pain inside us and what is causing them. Most of the programmes are created during childhood and become beliefs as we have not worked on them to release. It goes into our subconscious, and we live it every day without knowing that we have the power to reverse or release it.

> *Growth is painful, change is painful. But nothing is as painful as staying stuck somewhere you don't belong!*
>
> —Mandy Hale

This chapter will explore what is pain and why we feel pain pain. Any feeling that is of lower energy—and not for our highest and best (not in our best interest)—is an expression of pain like fear, anxiety, jealousy, hatred, resentment, guilt, and the like. The common feeling is "I am not enough," which is connected with a whole lot of other beliefs.

Going beyond the pain to discover the triggers and working on yourself to dissolve the feeling of pain is a process we need to work on every single day.

Tell me what is the pain you are living with?

I lived with a feeling of loneliness all my life. I felt lonely when I was never alone. From the time I was born, I have always received so much love, attention, and protection from my parents. I have always been treated like a princess in their lives and have always felt so loved. All my wishes would be granted even before I asked. I am blessed and privileged, but I still felt lonely. And this loneliness was related to multiple limiting beliefs inside me. My feeling of loneliness stemmed from my past life experiences and beliefs, which I discovered after going within and beyond this life. My past life belief was brought by my soul into my present life as I didn't do the work it takes to release it.

I achieved every kind of success, but my loneliness often took over and caused me to be in pain throughout my journey, and I never gave myself the chance to enjoy even the best moments of my life. My feelings of loneliness along with others took away my ability to cherish and celebrate life. I was living but not alive.

Similarly, there are feelings inside each one of us that make us feel disempowered in this journey. There could be a few feelings and beliefs or many intertwined feelings and beliefs. It is super important to start identifying them in order to become aware and start eliminating them.

The inability to realise the feelings coming from our beliefs and programming prolong our pain. Our soul creates beliefs from the time we are born and sometimes even before. And we live in this pain unaware of the reason and purpose of it.

When we understand the truth and start working on removing the layers we have put on through experiences, we start seeing the reality. The truth is and always will stand that the universe has our back, we are loved, we are enough, and we are powerful.

All we have to do is be the sculptor of our lives and chip away all that is not us. We have to keep digging inside us till we find the gold, which is the realisation.

My personal experience, combined with Joan Cusack Handler's article on identifying your feelings in Pyschologytoday.com, will give you great insights on how to identify the beliefs and your programming.

1. **Monitor your thought cycle.**

    - What feelings am I aware of having? (There are often many.)

    - What is the most prominent one? (Try to describe it to yourself. Also, don't be afraid to push yourself past answers like "fine" or "okay." Continue by asking what "fine" means. We often resist even our own probing.)

    - When did I become aware of this feeling?

I recommend having a notebook to record your questions and answers. Don't rush through it. Describe each feeling thoroughly and be sure to include pleasurable ones.

It's important to know what enhances your life; these are vital in providing some measure of balance when life is difficult.

These questions will lead to others and will likely take you to different places—perhaps ones you haven't travelled before. You may surprise yourself with details or memories that haven't been available before. Journaling these thoughts will shed light on some patterns.

2. **Identify your triggers.**

- What might be triggering this feeling?

- Is someone saying something hurting me? Why is it hurting me?

- What's happening (or not happening) in my daily life? (It helps to deconstruct one's day, week, or month.) Pay particular attention to events, thoughts, or dreams that you have no control of and perhaps have decided "not to pay attention to" because you cannot change them. This is a common pitfall. The fact that we have no control itself brings an emotional reaction.

- Perhaps your answer is, "I don't even know how I feel." One direction to take in this kind of situation is to examine your behaviour daily. This can help to tease out feelings not recognised initially.

So, ask yourself:

- How is my home life?

- Am I getting along with my partner? My children? My parents and siblings?

- How am I doing at work? Am I enjoying my work? Am I getting along with my coworkers? My boss? What are they telling about me and their feelings about me? Can I see validity in what they're saying?

Look for patterns that may be forming. Explore them. What do they tell you?

I remember a conversation I had with my husband, and I felt "He doesn't know me for who I am." Later that week I had a conversation with my father-in-law and ended up the same way; even after explaining myself, I felt he didn't know who I was. I took notice of the pattern, trying to release the pain in my morning meditation, I started digging, and the core belief was ego. The very fact I was getting triggered by these conversations and was feeling attacked; I had to ask myself multiple questions and dig deep to find out that my ego was being hurt. I then started working on what is ego and what is its purpose and how to let go of it.

My learning on "ego" from that episode was that we may think that if we are humble, if we are kind, and if we do not want expensive material objects, we have no ego; but ego exists deeper than we think.

It exists when we feel someone doesn't know "me" or when we feel they don't recognise/appreciate or love me for who "I" am.

"I" is the ego that exists within us. When we are not at all affected by people around us not recognising us and not loving us for who we are that's when the shift starts.

What matters is that we should be aware of who we are, means if we understand and appreciate ourself then what others think will not matter, and we then will have the courage to remain being who we want to be.

We are who we are for a reason, and when we become aware of that, we start embarking on our true journey and purpose. If you let ego be alive, you will lose your true purpose. Recognise ego, awaken to your reason to incarnate!

3. **Don't judge what you feel.**

Give names to your feelings and be specific and honest. "I don't have any reason to feel bad/anxiety or fear," you may say. Wait for an outcome before assuming the worst. We tend to criticise ourselves (as if feelings follow reason!). The reality is that life events generate feelings. They simply do. Though we may decide which feelings to attend to, we don't decide to feel or not feel. It's our project to identify them and give them room to breathe.

In another instance, I had to prepare for a presentation, and few nights before, I was terribly afraid. Public speaking is one of the most common phobias, ahead of death, spiders, or heights. Though I was confident that I would deliver it well, I felt fear; the opposite of fear is courage, and I knew I had to work on courage. In my morning session the next day, I started meditating to replace fear with courage and went deep into releasing fear on all levels. It took me a few days, but I was able to release it. We all have the ability to release the feelings that don't serve us; all we need is the awareness, the process, and the discipline to release it. We have to invest the time and do the work.

To explain, we feel fear on many fronts of life, and we can eliminate most of it by working on it every time it appears. Will discuss more on eliminating beliefs in the next chapter.

4. **Speak about your feelings.**

Vulnerability is a strength; we have to fully embrace ourselves, and once we do that, we are not worried of being exposed. The fact is that the more that we admit our feelings to ourselves and our loved ones, the more likely they are to diminish in size. The more stifled a feeling is, the greater its intensity. Feelings function like a pressure cooker: pressure increases without release. Then, once released, the intensity is reduced.

Finally, by way of reassurance, it's important to note that people are often afraid to face a feeling because of what it will lead to. They needn't be. Confronting a feeling is a very different thing than our response to it. These are two very separate realities. Contrary to what we may imagine, facing one's anger does not mean that we will act out on it and do something destructive. At this stage, it's important to identify the feelings; it's only when we identify our feelings that we are able to go deeper and get to the core belief in order to release it.

5. **Do you live in the now?**

This is a big one. We either live in the future or in the past, and that is one of the most challenging things to overcome in life. Most of us are saddened by our past experiences and lose faith and courage to change our reality in the now, or we fear the future based on our past and assume it to be as painful. We fail to realise that every day is a new day and we have the power to evolve and grow and better ourselves with every new minute. We have the power to change our thoughts and create a new reality.

A simple exercise helped me. Every time your thoughts sway either ways, catch them and bring them back to the now. If you consciously practise this exercise, soon you will start living in the now and feeling life in each and every cell of your body. Living in the now is being alive.

At thirty-one years, I felt my life was over. I was predicting my future based on my past. The twelve years of my life from age twenty-three to thirty-five were extremely challenging. From relationships to my business and to myself, nothing was as per my expectations. I was at my lowest point. Life seemed unfair; I felt like a victim, which made me predict my future. Though I had the hope of a better future, I couldn't see it and always lived in the future, unaware of the present. I was not doing anything to change my reality, energy, and thoughts. I was ignorant, and as a result, I always lived in pain.

If we live in the energy of the past, we will never be able to change our future.

—Meher

THE SAFE MODEL mentioned in the book *Solve for Happy* by Mo Gawdat clearly explains how to identify the feelings and get to the core of your belief. We must keep going until there is nothing more to discover.

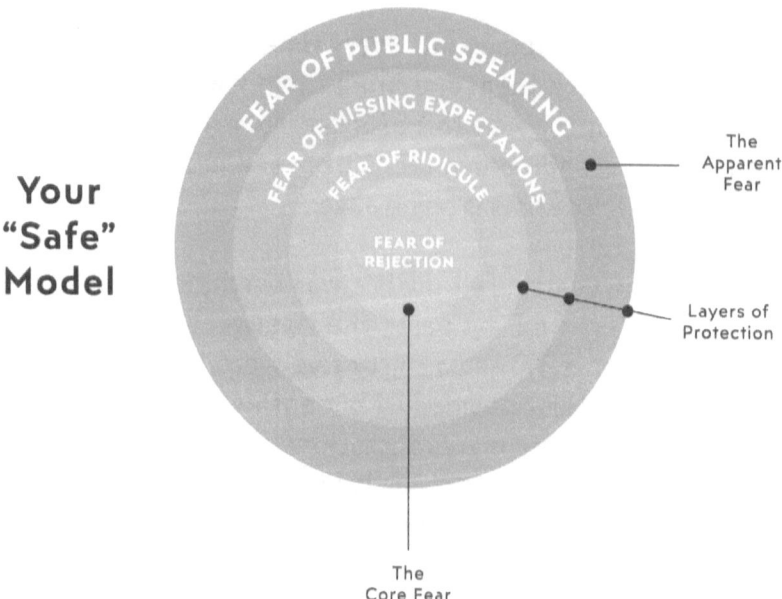

Your "Safe" Model

UNDERSTANDING PAIN

If you don't identify and work on elimination, your brain looks for every possible threat that may trigger it.

Identifying feelings is an important process in this journey; for this to work I need you to commit to me that you will follow the process. Make mental notes or physical notes, but you have to make notes and then sit in silence to dig deeper. Your life is yours to design, and I challenge you to face your feelings to liberate yourself.

If you are unable to identify and work on your beliefs on your own, please do not hesitate to seek guidance of coaches and healers. There is no shame in working on yourself with someone who has the expertise to do it. I have seen healers and coaches many times in these twelve years and continue to do so, if after several days of working on myself I can't get to the core belief. My life is my responsibility; no one else will show me the way. My evolution is my responsibility, and I work on it with the knowledge I have acquired. So don't be afraid of seeking external help to go through the above five steps with you, a healer or coach or an expert will be able to contribute to your journey if you are unable to do it alone.

The power for creating a better future is contained in the present moment: You create a good future by creating a good present.

—Eckhart Tolle

Now is all that we have and we must live in the now to experience life in its full form. Pain is an illusion of the mind; all the problems are an illusion of the mind. Once we are aware of the illusion that we have created, it is easier to dissolve it. By digging deep into the core issue, we are easily able to release the belief that is limiting us. When you put your mind to it, you can overcome pain.

From the time you get up tomorrow, I would like to request you to monitor your feelings—what are you feeling most of the time—and note some of them. Once you have named the feeling, it's time to go beyond and ask questions and start digging deeper. Also, identify the patterns that are created as a few feelings can have one core belief. You have to go past your brain's defense mechanism, and you will discover where the feeling stems from. Keep going until there is nothing more to discover. Name your beliefs and feelings.

If we don't go deep to the core of the issue, then the core belief will show up in another form. I worked very hard all these years to release and reverse beliefs, but the identification of lack of self-love didn't surface up until two years ago. Be patient and mindful when you work on your beliefs. Trust the process.

Once you have identified the feelings and narrowed down the core beliefs, it's time to start releasing them. There are several ways to release or reverse beliefs, and we will discover them in the next chapter. The aim has to be to dissolve them so they don't come back to you.

I was exhilarated by the new realisation that I could change the character of my life by changing my beliefs. I was instantly energised because I realised that there was a science-based path that would take me from my job as a perennial victim to my new position as a co-creator of my destiny

—Bruce Lipton

5
Reprogramming Yourself
Dissolving the Feeling along with the Beliefs

> *You are personally responsible for everything in your life. If you believe you are powerful, you are. And when you believe you are powerless, you are. You are what your beliefs are.*
>
> —Anonymous

BRUCE LIPTON MENTIONS that 80 percent of the audience that attend his events do not test positive on "I love myself" because of all the critical assessment they received as children. Though our parents correct and assess us to help us improve, what it does is create programmes of inadequacy and "I am not good enough" thoughts. So as adults we react and behave based on our fundamental programming of not loving ourself. This explains our belief clearly, and if we do not love ourselves, then how can we ever be in a loving relationship with anything or anyone?

What is a Belief?

A belief is a habit of mind in which trust or confidence is placed in some person or thing. It is accepted, considered to be true, and held as an opinion in you.

Most of our core beliefs are formed when we are children. We enter this world with a clean slate and without preconceived beliefs. Our inferences and what others tell us while growing up are imprinted in our subconscious and are held there.

Core beliefs are basic beliefs about ourselves, other people, and the world we live in. They are things we hold to be absolute truths deep down, underneath all our "surface" thoughts. Essentially, core beliefs determine how you perceive and interpret the world. I reiterate here that most of the time these beliefs are not created by our experiences but by how our mind perceives other's attitudes, opinions, and thoughts communicated to us and what they tell us.

The way that these beliefs are created is that they are based on your parents', grandparents', or family's perceptions, and they do not always serve you. When we are in adulthood it is important for us to evaluate what beliefs we hold and how they serve us.

The awareness that reprogramming our beliefs will change our lives is what we need to live fuller and happier lives. And what follows is ways to reprogramme our system to lead a fulfilled life.

If you could be anybody, who would you be?

Many of us think, imagine, and feel that if we were somebody else, we would be happier, more successful, and more content with life.

In this chapter you will learn that we don't need to be that somebody; we are who we are meant to be. And we can achieve all that we want to by being ourselves. We are here for a reason and we are here to learn, to evolve, and to flourish. There is no destination; we are here to enjoy this journey, and it's an eternal journey of joy.

This is being human! All we need to do is break free from the beliefs that limit us to achieve our greatness.

Beliefs are built in childhood and sometimes go beyond lives. Hence it is very important to recognise them from recurring patterns of feelings and programming right from the early days in order to reverse/release or dissolve them. At the age of thirty all I wanted to do was to be reborn to live a life I desired and had imagined as a little girl. I was in a prison in my head, not knowing how to get freedom. **Freedom** is the ability, the courage, and the drive to be better every single day. This has nothing to do with anyone else; it is related to the feeling inside you. As a young couple married at an early age, my expectations were created by the beliefs of a Disney movie that I was unable to dissolve. This left me in despair.

The other strong programmes that I discovered along my journey are of expectation and attachment. The deep understanding of them and releasing them shifted my life to another level.

Expectation. As a child I was loved beyond measure and protected. My parents called me princess all my life and treated me like one. My expectation of being treated like a princess, given the love I had experienced in my childhood, was not wrong. But because I was married at an early age, I was unable to transit into that phase and my expectation of receiving the same love and attention didn't serve me in adulthood. It's a natural process of life; you are supposed to grow up and not expect the same from your husband as you become the mother (metaphorically) and it's then your responsibility to give that love. It was very challenging for me to adjust to the understanding that my husband is not meant to give me the same love as my parents.

Once I understood this I reprogrammed it to "I love, live, and give with no expectations from another," but of course this expectation was also derived from the core belief of not loving myself. So I had to work on both simultaneously.

Attachment. This is one of the five vices in Hinduism; it is called *moh*, and as it is said, attachment doesn't serve us. Attachment to anything worldly—possessions, relations, and status—is a cause of sorrow. We are here on this earth as passengers in transit, and hence to be attached to anything that you cannot take to your afterlife hinders your evolution and growth. I was very attached to my husband and to my business, and that actually suffocated me because when you are attached you expect, and then it's a result-driven outcome. What I learned is that I must strive for the best on all fronts of life but not be attached to the outcome. It means we should sincerely work on our path but without the desire and attachment to the outcome. Letting go of our **attachment** to the **outcome** is freeing. It helps us to be more present with the doing, the being, the act itself, rather than what might come in the future. It helps us to enjoy the journey rather than waiting for the destination.

There is not one path but many to dissolve and release beliefs. My introduction to beliefs was when a dear friend introduced me to Theta Healing, and I started learning about the biology of beliefs and its impact on our life at the genetic, past life, and soul levels. I knew I had to learn this in order to become free of the beliefs that were not serving me. I did eight different levels and became a healer and a teacher.

Theta Healing helped me dissolve a lot of beliefs, and I started living a better life. Like every skill and learning, we need practice to get better. To be honest, I practised it, but I was not consistent with it. As the old age saying goes, "practice makes perfect." To improve your life you have to do the work. I did some work but not every single day, and hence one belief was not dissolved. While I felt better and lived a better life in my head, something was still off. Though I was viewed as an achiever, a successful, strong, and a beautiful woman—I didn't see myself this way because I still held the belief of not being in love with myself.

Your beliefs become your thoughts
Your thoughts become your words
Your words become your action
Your actions become your habits
Your habits become your values
Your values become your destiny

—Bruce Lipton

Here I draw upon the learning from Dr. Joe Dispenza and Dr. Bruce Lipton, who have immensely helped me become me. Even after practising Theta Healing on and off for about ten years, I was unable to feel life and be alive. For me, being alive is being in love. Being in love with everything as it is in the now and living in faith. Faith is unwavering trust in the universe and its forces, in other words in my spiritual master. I wasn't feeling this because I didn't do the work I needed to. Success is a result of consistent practice, and that's what I didn't do. It's when I came across the work of these two great men, my life started evolving.

If you want a new outcome, you will have to break the habit of being yourself and reinvent a new self—and that new self is actually your soul self. Beliefs, experiences, and circumstances make us something we are not, and then we lose the power to reinvent or reconnect with ourselves, to become how we were meant to be in the first place. And that's exactly what happened to me. My circumstances made me lose all the power to become who I was meant to be, and only after I started the below practices, I gained my power back because these are the practices that can help you dissolve your beliefs.

1. **Meditation.** Meditation is a means to move beyond your analytic mind, so you can access your subconscious mind as that's where the magic begins. When we sit in meditation, we reason out our thoughts and feelings and dig deep to release them. Most of the time it happens on its own. Meditation empowers you to become more you. It is a way to get in touch with your higher self, your soul self, to see the love you have inside you for you. This is the most important practice we must commit to. While I was doing everything else to be me, the only thing I didn't do is meditate, and hence I met myself and fell in love with myself only two years ago.

I would like to elaborate and explain the difference between meditation and mindfulness.

Mindfulness is the awareness of "some-thing," while **meditation is** the awareness of "no-thing."

Meditation is a large umbrella term that encompasses the practice of reaching the ultimate consciousness and concentration to acknowledge the mind and, in a way, self-regulate it. It can involve a lot of techniques or practices to reach this heightened level of consciousness—including compassion, love, patience, and, of course, mindfulness.

Mindfulness is a type of meditation, alongside tantra, yoga, silence, breathing, and emptiness. Mindfulness is the act of focusing on being in the present, such as focusing completely on drinking a hot cup of tea, taking in its scent, warmth, and taste, and removing overpowering emotions from the mind.

To learn more about meditation I would propose to read and hear the learning of Emily Fletcher's message on meditation.

2. **Reprogramming.** Your subconscious mind runs the show; however positive we are, unless we don't work to change the programming in our subconscious mind, it will not work. Positive thinking is part of our creative process that comes from the conscious mind; hence we don't see a difference in outcome because we are not aligning it with our subconscious mind. And subconscious mind can be reprogrammed in the Theta state, which is just before we are falling asleep as our conscious mind is shutting off. This is where we can use affirmations or programming audios, so it goes straight to subconscious while we sleep. The fact that we are 95 percent controlled by our subconscious mind and only 5 percent by our conscious mind is something we need to consider all the time as that is the main factor in shaping our reality and destiny.

3. **Learning.** When we commit ourselves to learn new information every single day, we biologically wire that information to our cerebral architecture. And this new information helps us view life, circumstances, and feelings from a new perspective. When we have new perspectives, we make informed choices of our thoughts and actions. Learning is for the mind what air is for your body. Learning is extremely important because when you know better you can do better.

4. **Gratitude.** Gratitude is one of the most powerful emotions for increasing your level of energy. It teaches

your body emotionally that the event you're grateful for has already happened, because we usually give thanks after a desirable event has occurred. If you bring up the emotion of gratitude before the actual event, your body (as the unconscious mind) will begin to believe that the future event has indeed already happened—or is happening to you in the present moment. Gratitude, therefore, is the ultimate state of receivership. It's your elevated energy that will attract the outcome you desire.

5. **Repetition.** Practice is where most of us lag behind; we make a commitment to ourselves but fail to keep it. What we need is practising all of this every single day to make an impact on our lives. Through repetition we create habits; this is the way to acquire subconscious programmes after seven years of age. Repetition helps reprogramme the subconscious; hence it is imperative we continue the practices of all of the above.

6. **Journaling.** Journaling is super important for me as it helps me to work on the above areas and more. After I journal my gratitude, I also journal my thoughts, my feelings, and what I would like to work on next. It helps me release any stress or negativity and give forgiveness to myself and anyone I have felt hurt by. Just the act of putting the first thoughts in the morning on a paper makes me start my day with energy. Journaling consciously helps us work on the areas that need upgrade, and through the above practices we can do the work to reprogramme our subconscious. Journaling gives structure and direction to our personal goals.

What you need to know is that you cannot attract positivity and anything to your life until you don't change your energy by changing your beliefs, which changes your feelings. And this will only happen when you commit to practising the six steps to evolution every single day. The day you don't take a shower, you will feel sweaty and sticky and smelly. You will not feel fresh, and the same goes with the mind. To transform, you have to connect to yourself every single day.

My energy started changing once I was reprogramming through the practice of meditation, learning, exercise, journaling, and repetition. I was consistently focussed in the now. My determination to practise all of my rituals moved me higher and helped me evolve. And all that was not me was being chipped away. The more I was being me, the more in love I was falling with myself, gaining power, and feeling limitless and fulfilled. I have always wanted to live in the honeymoon phase forever, and this was coming true as I was consciously working on reprogramming my subconscious mind.

Practice makes perfect, and success is something you attract by the person you become. Remember, you have the key to unlock the door to being you and change your reality.

In conclusion, I highly recommend hearing and reading the findings of Bruce Lipton on the Honeymoon effect. The Honeymoon effect is a state of bliss, passion, energy, and health resulting from a huge love. Your life is so beautiful that you can't wait to get up to start a new day and thank the universe. This is something you can always remain in once you are aware and practise consciously to reprogramme your conscious mind. This is how I would like you to feel every single day once you have started reprogramming your beliefs of inadequacy, fear, pain, and lack of love. You will become more you because you will realise that all of these were illusions. None of this holds true to your soul self. You are complete, loved, courageous, and beautiful. The next chapter will deepen you being you and help you letting go of everything that you are not and everything that is not serving you. Welcome to phase four!

Respect yourself enough to walk away from anything that no longer serves you, grows you, or makes you happy.

—Robert Tew

6
Serving Your Soul
Letting Go

In the process of letting go, you will lose many things from the past, but you will find yourself.

—Deepak Chopra

LET GO TO be you! I am happy to see you here, reading this chapter, and extremely proud that by reading this book you have started your transformational journey. Evolution is what life is all about; and the more you evolve, the more fulfilled you will feel. By letting go of thoughts, habits, things, people, and activities that no longer serve you, you will be liberated!

Free yourself from being controlled by what other people think. Start to prioritise how you feel about yourself. As

Mahatma Gandhi said, "Happiness is when what you think, what you say, and what you do are in harmony." You can't live by your values if you're living for the approval of others.

Leave who you were,
Love who you are,
Look forward to
Who you will become...

In this chapter, I will share with you all that I let go of and the happiness it brought me. The more you let go, the more you become you. Letting go gets you closer to the seat of your soul and also brings immense courage to your being. You meet your authentic self.

At first, letting go will feel very uncomfortable, because you are used to certain things, you are used to spending time in a certain way, and you are used to attending certain events. However, when you weigh the pros and cons of letting go, you will discover peace beyond what I can express.

As I mentioned in the previous chapter, you have to break the habit of being you if you want a new outcome. We are addicted to thinking and feeling a certain way. We have to break the addiction of our past thoughts and feelings. And it is those habits we have to let go of in order to align ourself with our soul and be the powerful, limitless being we are.

Nothing changes if we don't determine to change it; remember it is up to us to live the best version of our life every single day. We become comfortable and accept our current state without realising that life starts beyond our comfort zone. A comfort zone is a psychological state of mind in which things feel familiar to a person and they are at ease. This saying holds true only when you step outside your comfort zone and when you find out new things about yourself that you didn't know. And by experiencing parts of life that you haven't experienced before. Pushing yourself to perform your best every single day is what will bring you the experience you desire to live a life of fulfilment.

We are not a victim of anything but our own thinking. I felt like a victim of my circumstances for thirteen years. I felt it was karma that I didn't have the power to live my life on my terms. A victim mentality or belief is actually a way to avoid taking any responsibility for yourself or your life. By believing that you have no power, you don't take action. It is when you blame your circumstances and people around you for your challenges that make your pain justified. You blame someone or the other for everything that is wrong in your life; however, this is also more in your head than in reality. You see the negative effect of every challenging situation not the positive.

I felt like the victim of my past life, I felt a victim of my karma, I felt a victim of my father and of my husband. I believed life was happening to me and I couldn't do anything about it, but that was because I was not aware and I was not doing anything to become aware.

I believed my life was to live in pain, I believed it was my destiny to live an unfulfilled life. Imagine how horrible that was. I was below a five on each and every aspect of my wheel of life (Refer Page 75). I had given up to my challenges vs. believing I had the power to change my life.

Once I started letting go of my beliefs, I started feeling lighter; it was like a weight being lifted off from my shoulder. I had constant body pain, either in my legs or in my shoulder, and once my transformation started, everything was gone. Our physical ailments and pains are a reflection of our emotional state of being. My body was in constant pain and now 10 years later I feel renewed energy every single day. My health is in perfect condition.

After we reprogramme and start letting go of beliefs there is more to let go of—letting go of our old habits, our thought patterns, material things, people, and conversations that don't serve us. You have started work on your inner being, and now it's time to work on your personality. It's about aligning the thoughts with the actions.

Get ready to let go.

1. **Habits.** We have to let go of a few habits and also create a few new ones. We have many habits that hinder our thoughts and growth. Let me share a few: I had a habit of checking my phone as soon as I woke up. I replaced that with my morning ritual, which is meditation, journaling, gratitude, reading, and dropping my kids to school. Only after which, I check my messages and emails. I didn't exercise as I believed I had no time. I created a new habit of exercising at least three times

a week if not more. I wanted a healthier me. I created habits that would serve me and keep my energy elevated consistently.

2. **Thoughts.** We often think about things that we have no control of and things that do not serve our being the best version of ourself. As mentioned previously, I would constantly think about the destination of my fashion brand and how will I get there, without working on myself in the now. We all have the basic values and knowledge and education to make us successful entrepreneurs, but we don't simultaneously work on ourself. And that is something which I was unaware of. All I did was worry about the future and be saddened by the past. All my thoughts were related to events in my past and dreams of the future. Once I let go of the worries in both these parts of my life, I started coming alive. I had to let go of the past completely till I didn't feel anything at all. And I had to let go of my thoughts of the future to live today. This needs practice and exercises. I would often write (gratitude and journal), read, or meditate to avoid any thoughts that were not serving me. We have to become the observer of our thoughts to see the drama our mind creates and then divert it. We must remember we are the master of our thoughts and not the other way around.

3. **Things.** I realised a lot of my time was taken up by shopping and online shopping and arranging the things I already have. I took to the concept of minimalism

where I didn't buy anything for twelve months consciously. I gave up on buying things that I didn't absolutely need and started giving away the things that I no longer used or needed. I adapted to a minimal way of life. This helped me focus my mind on what was most important for my evolution as a human, a mother, and an entrepreneur. And it also created new habits.

4. **People.** As you become aware, you will start getting intuitive and start feeling energies; your intellect will prompt you to spending your time most wisely to be the best version of yourself. When I was in this phase a lot of the people I would connect with faded away and new people with new energies came into my life who were appreciating and valuing me for my soul self and helping me be more me. This is an amazing experience, and I wish you this phase as soon as possible. I have fewer connections and relations with people, and that helps me value and appreciate those with similar energies, and I feel we are growing together.

5. **Activities.** There are always things we do to stay in the limelight, I like to say. However, when the limelight is not important then the activities connected with these will diminish automatically, and you must embrace this. I used to socialise and dine out at least three times a week, which would get me about six hours of sleep. When I didn't have the morning rituals, I was completely fine but as soon as I started my morning routines, I realised that the quality of my

meditation is not as strong as the day I was sleeping on time and being home. I started letting go of my dinner/party and event nights. That doesn't mean I don't enjoy dancing and music and social gatherings; it just means you choose more wisely where and when you spend your time.

Changing habits and letting go is the most challenging part of this journey, and you may fall back into your old self. To be able to defeat your old self you have to make sure you strengthen your new self every single day by creating and adhering to the new habits. You are here to be the best version of yourself. To be living a life of power, courage, and love, let not anything come in its way. In this earth school, the ones doing the work will perform the best when exams are due. The ones prepared will improve and grow with every challenging situation that comes their way. This earth school is far more rewarding than when we were in school growing up, so we have to be prepared and do the work. We must leave this world with flying colours and a legacy to be remembered.

What we learned here is that we have to distance ourself from everything that doesn't raise us higher in our journey, and that is everything from thoughts, habits, people, things, and activities. Time is super precious, and we need to recognise and realise that. Being you is the most important task of your life; you are here for greatness and to experience the magic. Always remember, success is something you attract by the person you become, and your personal growth will always supersede your professional achievements. Be focussed, live it, and love it.

To be in love with yourself, you have to let go of everything that doesn't serve you, and don't be afraid of letting go. Everything that you are doing is getting you closer to being you, and when you are you, you will feel nothing less than a superman/superwoman. I love being and feeling like a superwoman, and I am sure you will love it too. Life feels like it's in a state of flow.

I challenge you to identify and let go of one thing in each of the above categories on completion of this chapter.

The final process is you being in love with yourself for who you are, and I am excited for you to feel this with me in the next chapter. I welcome you to feeling what I feel every single day. A world of bliss, equanimity, sublimeness, and transcendence awaits you!

Reference:

The **Wheel of Life** is based on the notion that there are specific categories that form the cornerstone of your overall **life** experience. The **wheel** helps you to better understand which of your **life** areas are flourishing and which ones need the most work. Join the dots between segments and review using the questions below:

SERVING YOUR SOUL

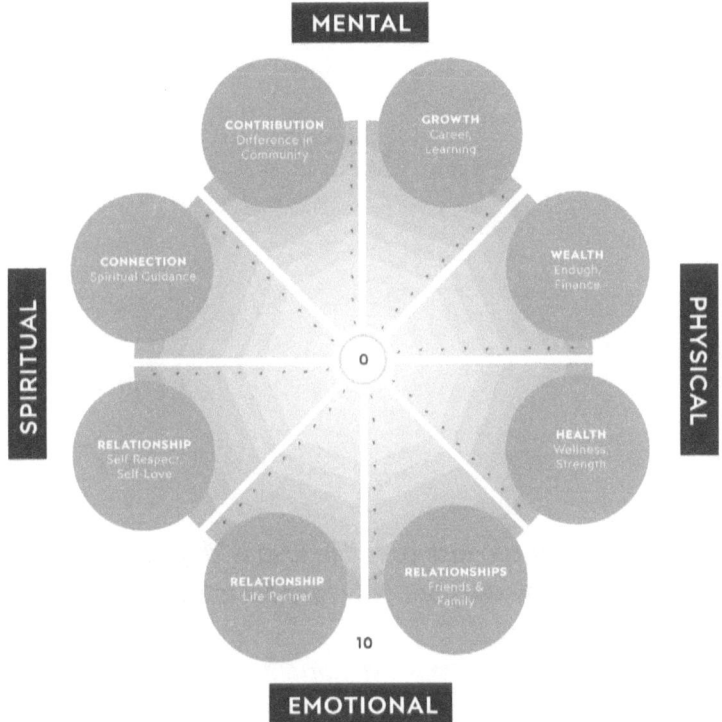

Source: The Wheel of Life from https://www.peopleconnexion.com/news/wheel-of-life-exercise/45639/

Give the below a go!

- Does this surprise you?
- Which areas are higher than you thought?
- Which areas are lower than you thought?
- Does this line up with what you value?
- Which areas are most important to you?
- How can you make changes to improve those areas?
- What changes can you make in the next three months in two of those areas?
- Who can you share your commitment with?

*It's never too late to fall in love with yourself,
you are your only faithful lover!*

—Meher

7
Be in Love
Love Yourself Fearlessly

A man who is master of himself can end a sorrow as he can invent a pleasure. I don't want to be at the mercy of my emotions. I want to use them, to enjoy them, and to dominate them.

—*Oscar Wilde*

LOVE HAS NOTHING to do with someone else. It is all about you. It is the way of being. It is your own quality. It is already within you. You are Love!

In this chapter we will discuss Love, and how it feels to be in love with yourself. Once you have read, understood, and practised the steps in the last four chapters you should be ready to feel love.

I want you to dust away all that you are not and see yourself from the perspective of the divine.

You can change any relationship right now by changing your perspective of seeing the things you love, appreciate, and are grateful for in the other person, and the same applies to you. It's not about how the world makes you feel; it's about what you give yourself and what you feel. It's about seeing yourself as enough, full, and complete.

All I ever wanted to feel is love from my husband, and my inner conflict on perspective of love saw no resolution until I didn't realise, acknowledge, and become aware that I am not giving love to myself. Once I started loving myself, I had no complaints and it actually reversed. Now my husband teases me that I don't love him, so it's a great shift in our relationship.

Earlier, when I didn't love myself, I didn't receive and accept compliments as if there was a block in my heart. I would never thank the person who paid the compliment because I couldn't absorb it. Now, I feel the love I am given, and I am grateful for it and convey the same. I feel the love not only from family and friends but also from stakeholders in our business and all business relationships. I express my sincere love and gratitude to everyone in my life, and I equally receive love!

Miracles happen when you start making the shift to admiring, appreciating, and loving yourself.

You now know the core of the issue within you and have the tools to work on each of those elements to eliminate and dissolve the pain, the beliefs, and everything that doesn't serve you.

Now I want you to fall in love with yourself and be in love with yourself forever. I am sure you will agree, love is forever.

You are divine, and you are here to create magic; close your eyes, take a deep breath, and feel it!

Below exercises will help you further feel the love; you will need your journal for this.

1. **Write down ten things you appreciate about yourself.**
   It can be as tiny as saying please every time you say something. I will share with you, when I say please and thank you to my house staff, they often tell me that I don't have to say that; however, I still believe that it is extremely important to give respect to everyone and I continue to use a lot of please and thank you. So, for example, I appreciate my kindness to my staff. Please carry on.

2. **Write down ten things you admire about yourself.**
   This can be the physical aspect of you. Like, I admire my hair, I admire my eyes, and so on. Please don't be shy. Be a lover of yourself. By admiring yourself you are giving gratitude to God for creating a beautiful you. And remember that to receive more of anything you have to give thanks in advance.

3. **Write down ten things that you are proud of.**
   These can be achievements like closing a contract or helping your child ace an exam or finding out a great deal on a workout class. Feel free and proud. You are God's creation of an intelligent and smart human, and you possess everything to be proud of.

4. **Write a love letter to yourself.**
   Pour out your heart and express the love you have ever wanted to feel. You owe this to yourself. Be in love with yourself, every bit of yourself; feel every word you pen. Make it as detailed and as expressive as you can. Love yourself for who you are.

   Here's my first love letter to myself:

   > I love you because you live authentically. You are focused on creating a life with meaning.
   > Your burning desire to constantly improve yourself to be the best version of yourself is a service to your soul and people connected to you. The more evolve, the more your can serve humanity & family.
   > I love you because you have built your muscle, stretched yourself to live a life of fulfillment by attending to all areas of your life.
   > I love you so much because you are seeking and working towards your purpose to incarnate. I am proud of who you have become & I am excited to see you develope further.

   THE POWER OF WRITING 13

If you have embraced the theory in this book and the previous chapters, then these exercises should be fulfilling. These should add the smile I am looking for, and your heart should beat how it did/does when you met your lover for the first time.

For anything to work, you have to work on yourself. By reading this book and keeping it aside, nothing will change; the books you read and the habits you create, create you. If you have followed and practised the exercises in the previous chapter, this is the icing on the cake.

To transform yourself, you have to be committed, have to be disciplined, and have to want it! The universe conspires to give you what you want when you align yourself with its energies. And the energy of the universe is love! You were born from love, into love, and we go back to love; so let's live in love.

Be driven by faith rather than fear; both cannot be seen.

Self-love is the process of knowing yourself, connecting with your inner self, overcoming the self-limiting beliefs, letting go of everything that doesn't serve you, and falling in love with yourself. Fall in love with yourself for who you are! You can only be in love with someone if you know them and remain connected to them all the time, you spend time with them, you share your vulnerabilities with them, and you confide in them. This is the relationship of love and trust that I would like to create with yourself. It is not selfish to focus on your personal development. Self-love elevates you to a higher being, and selfishness is the act of thinking about your personal benefit.

> *Self-love is the unshakable belief in the worthiness of your own self. It is a matter of knowing, understanding, and honouring your value. If you are searching for love, know this well. Love will not come to you if you don't love yourself. In self-love you are a giver. A giver is not a beggar. You cannot give and beg at the same time.*
>
> —Dr. Navana Kundu

I invite you to begin this exercise right after your meditation tomorrow morning; it will take about fifteen minutes. You can do these exercises as part of your daily journaling and repeat them as many times as you wish. The more love you bring to your being, the more you will evolve; and as your energy becomes love, you will attract everything that will serve you to lead a fulfilled and peaceful life.

Appreciate, Admire, Be Proud of yourself. You are your only faithful lover. Operate with love, bringing love into your being, and see the magic that awaits you!

This leads us to the conclusion of the book, and I am excited to share with you how I feel being alive as I didn't even know how dead I was until I came alive. I am grateful to be given this opportunity to write, and I am grateful that you have read my book. My purpose in life is to help release and dissolve the pain in you so you do not live a single day in pain anymore. My reward is your love towards yourself.

To be Alive is to be in Love, To be in love with yourself for who you are!

—Meher

8
Conclusion
Come Alive
Experience the Love in You

*Those who were seen dancing were called crazy
by those who could not hear the music.*

—Friedrich Nietzsche

THE MUSIC OF life is waiting to play on your tunes, please don't delay.

Your whole idea about yourself is borrowed—borrowed from those who have no idea of who they are themselves. All the pain is an illusion, and you have the power to release it. The power of creating a better future is contained in the present moment; you create a better future by creating a great present. Whatever the present moment, embrace it as if you have chosen it yourself. The present is all you have, live in the now. Eckhart Tolle is another great teacher who has helped me come alive through his teachings, and I remember them every waking moment.

Being alive is the realisation of your true self, of who you are. It is an inner experience in which you know that you are not only just enough, but you are always more than enough. That means there is nothing that exists or is in your life that can stop you from your true fulfilment. We are here to experience this life in all its glory. It is the knowing that who you are overcomes all things that could ever challenge you. It is an understanding that you are complete. This is something you already know inside of you, and it will come to surface the more connected you are to yourself.

I didn't even know I was dead until I came alive; this life is a gift to us and to treat it as one is our responsibility. Be courageous to live and rule by your heart. You are a divine being, and don't let anyone overrule your power—not even yourself.

Remember, everything in life is yours to have as long as you want it. What you seek is seeking you always. Walking on this path of life, you acquire and adorn feelings and beliefs that are not yours in the first place. Dissolving them to polish you to bring out your soul self is a mission to conquer. Once you let go and release yourself from the energies and the earthly materialistic things, people, and activities that no longer serve, you see the miracle happen.

CONCLUSION

I am grateful to be given this opportunity to share my learning and contribute to awaken you. I will highlight the five-phase process of self-love and my experience of being in Love and being Alive.

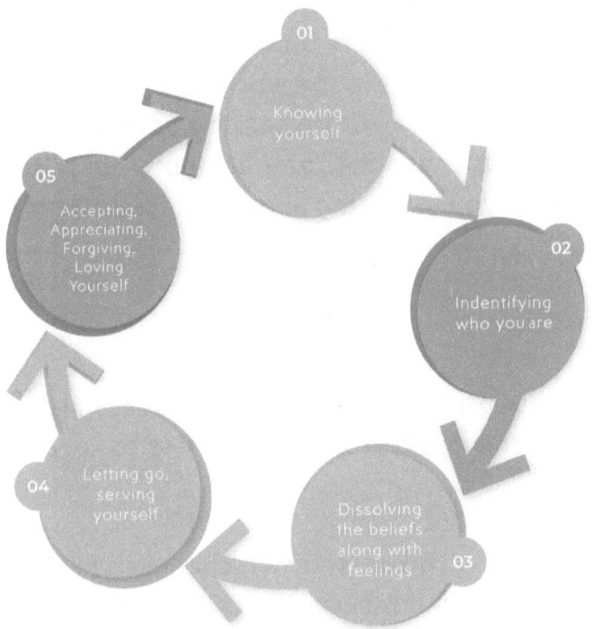

Your purpose is to exercise your truth of being, and what is your truth of being? It is to feel love in each and every cell of your body. And to be in love with life and yourself and everything as it is in the now. To be grateful for being who you are, to forgive and live in faith.

To be on the seat of your soul is paramount as that is when you gain authentic power. It's when we forget that we are both a Living Soul and a personality that the challenge arises. The conscious link between these two aspects of ourself is the most important discovery of our incarnation as humans. In the education system, at home, and in church you are taught about your personality—about your body, feelings, moods, desires, and thoughts—so you are unable to experience yourself as a Living Soul, as a spiritual entity apart from and beyond the personality. And my mission along with the many other great gurus in the world is to bring this to light. We cannot live a fulfilled life serving only the personality. Hence, the awareness that you are pure consciousness is what will shift you and bring about your transformation.

The five-phase process will serve you to start your transformation.

The five-phase process becomes effortless as much as you do it and what remain is few simple exercises to keep you in the zone of love.

1. **Meeting with Yourself.** My schedule is blocked for the first hour with meeting myself every single day! This is my meditation and connection with myself and the universe. I am the most important thing to me.

2. **Nurturing and Nourishing Yourself.** I eat what suits my body and exercise for an hour at least three days a week. Exercise keeps me healthy and fit so I can focus on all areas of my life fully. It gives me an increased level of energy and reduces the probability of me falling ill. The relation of health to mind is that most of our thoughts revolve around our physical and emotional well-being, and if this is taken care of then you

are able to focus on greater thoughts and things to do to become a better version of yourself.

3. **Learning and Reading.** I learn as if I am to live forever. I spend an hour a day either learning a new skill set or a new subject. I am a student of the earth school. If we are not prepared in the earth school with the knowledge we need to run our lives, then we are sure to fail.

4. **Writing and Journaling.** At the moment, I am doing the five-minute gratitude journal by Alex Ikonn. My journaling consists of love letters and gratitude to myself, my family, and my friends. I also do forgiveness journaling—it's forgiving myself and anyone who I had a negative charge with. **Forgiveness** is the intentional and voluntary process by which we undergo a change in feelings and attitude regarding an offense and overcome negative emotions such as resentment and vengeance. Forgiveness is an attribute of the Godly or of the saintly; when we are able to forgive, we shift to the next level of our evolution. It is an act done to release you from the bind of karma and keep you free from anticipation of revenge and its energy. Forgiveness is one of the most crucial practices of our journey.

We are on this beautiful journey called life, and we are here to enjoy it and cherish it with our full being. We are work in progress; let's not judge ourselves but keep learning and being aware so we grow to become a better version of ourself every single day. We must evolve in our words, actions, and thoughts to be who we are meant to be. It's a process. Let's embrace it and live it with love.

Once you have completed this book go to www.mehermirchandani.com and download all the free resources to continue your inward journey.

- I request you to take the self-love assessment on my site and evaluate where you stand in your journey. This will enable you to focus on areas that need more nurturing with more love.

- I have a daily journal that you can download from my site and use it to guide you through the five steps to Come Alive. A few pages are included at the end of the book to get you started.

- I also want you to make a promise to me to love yourself, no matter what. You have nothing to prove to anybody; the more you love yourself, the more love you will be able to give others.

- I want you to commit to a ritual to spend time with yourself every single day to be connected with who you are, without which none of this will be possible. I have been so powerless in my life that I really want my experience to be a learning to my readers. Everything we do is like a muscle we build; please stretch yourself to build strength in all areas of your being. Never give up! I know you have the power to be who you are meant to be.

CONCLUSION

Being Alive is Being in Love. You cannot lose it and it cannot leave you. The universe experiences itself through you for a brief moment called life. You are the universe in all its glory; celebrate yourself for who you are! And my mission is to evoke the transformation in you so that you are able to celebrate yourself every single moment!

Congratulations to you on completion of this book. Please celebrate and embrace yourself for this achievement. Please be proud of yourself at the commitment to growing yourself!

Come Alive Now!

If we are the same person before and after we loved, that means we haven't loved enough.

—Shafak, *Forty Rules of Love*

Happy Journaling

It all starts with you.
Love,
Meher

DATE __/__/20__

Our highest priority is to protect our ability to prioritise.
—Greg McKeown

I am grateful for
1. _____
2. _____
3. _____

I admire/appreciate/am proud of myself
1. _____
2. _____
3. _____

I learnt today/yesterday
1. _____
2. _____

Made me feel truly ALIVE,
☐ Meditation/silence _____
☐ Exercise/yoga/dance _____
☐ Reading _____
☐ _____

Daily affirmations, I am . . .
_____
_____

How will I make today great?
_____
_____

DATE __/__/20__

Whatever you think the world is withholding from you, you are withholding from the world.
—Ekhart Tolle

I am grateful for
1. _____
2. _____
3. _____

I admire/appreciate/am proud of myself
1. _____
2. _____
3. _____

I learnt today/yesterday
1. _____
2. _____

Made me feel truly ALIVE,
☐ Meditation/silence _____
☐ Exercise/yoga/dance _____
☐ Reading _____
☐ _____

Daily affirmations, I am . . .
_____
_____

How will I make today great?
_____
_____

DATE __/__/20__

*Darkness cannot drive out darkness: only light can do that.
Hate cannot drive out hate: only love can do that.*
—Martin Luther King Jr.

I am grateful for
1. _____
2. _____
3. _____

I admire/appreciate/am proud of myself
1. _____
2. _____
3. _____

I learnt today/yesterday
1. _____
2. _____

Made me feel truly ALIVE,
☐ Meditation/silence _____
☐ Exercise/yoga/dance _____
☐ Reading _____
☐ _____

Daily affirmations, I am . . .
_____
_____

How will I make today great?
_____
_____

DATE __/__/20__

Live as if you were to die tomorrow. Learn as if you were to live forever.
—Mahatma Gandhi

I am grateful for
1. _____
2. _____
3. _____

I admire/appreciate/am proud of myself
1. _____
2. _____
3. _____

I learnt today/yesterday
1. _____
2. _____

Made me feel truly ALIVE,
☐ Meditation/silence _____
☐ Exercise/yoga/dance _____
☐ Reading _____
☐ _____

Daily affirmations, I am . . .
_____
_____

How will I make today great?
_____
_____

DATE __/__/20__

No one can make you feel inferior without your consent.
—Eleanor Roosevelt

I am grateful for
1. _____
2. _____
3. _____

I admire/appreciate/am proud of myself
1. _____
2. _____
3. _____

I learnt today/yesterday
1. _____
2. _____

Made me feel truly ALIVE,
☐ Meditation/silence _____
☐ Exercise/yoga/dance _____
☐ Reading _____
☐ _____

Daily affirmations, I am . . .
_____
_____

How will I make today great?
_____
_____

DATE __/__/20__

Be yourself; everyone else is already taken.
—Oscar Wilde

I am grateful for
1. _____
2. _____
3. _____

I admire/appreciate/am proud of myself
1. _____
2. _____
3. _____

I learnt today/yesterday
1. _____
2. _____

Made me feel truly ALIVE,
☐ Meditation/silence _____
☐ Exercise/yoga/dance _____
☐ Reading _____
☐ _____

Daily affirmations, I am . . .
_____
_____

How will I make today great?
_____
_____

Beauty begins the moment you decide to be yourself.
—Coco Chanel

A love letter to myself

DATE __/__/20__

Be the change that you wish to see in the world.
—Mahatma Gandhi

I am grateful for
1. _____
2. _____
3. _____

I admire/appreciate/am proud of myself
1. _____
2. _____
3. _____

I learnt today/yesterday
1. _____
2. _____

Made me feel truly ALIVE,
☐ Meditation/silence _____
☐ Exercise/yoga/dance _____
☐ Reading _____
☐ _____

Daily affirmations, I am . . .
_____
_____

How will I make today great?
_____
_____

DATE __/__/20__

We accept the love we think we deserve.
—Stephen Chbosky

I am grateful for
1. _____
2. _____
3. _____

I admire/appreciate/am proud of myself
1. _____
2. _____
3. _____

I learnt today/yesterday
1. _____
2. _____

Made me feel truly ALIVE,
☐ Meditation/silence _____
☐ Exercise/yoga/dance _____
☐ Reading _____
☐ _____

Daily affirmations, I am . . .
_____
_____

How will I make today great?
_____
_____

DATE __/__/20__

There are only two ways to live your life. One is as though nothing is a miracle. The other is as though everything is a miracle.
—Albert Einstein

I am grateful for
1. _____
2. _____
3. _____

I admire/appreciate/am proud of myself
1. _____
2. _____
3. _____

I learnt today/yesterday
1. _____
2. _____

Made me feel truly ALIVE,
☐ Meditation/silence _____
☐ Exercise/yoga/dance _____
☐ Reading _____
☐ _____

Daily affirmations, I am . . .
_____
_____

How will I make today great?
_____
_____

DATE __/__/20__

It is never too late to be what you might have been.
—George Eliot

I am grateful for
1. _____
2. _____
3. _____

I admire/appreciate/am proud of myself
1. _____
2. _____
3. _____

I learnt today/yesterday
1. _____
2. _____

Made me feel truly ALIVE,
☐ Meditation/silence _____
☐ Exercise/yoga/dance _____
☐ Reading _____
☐ _____

Daily affirmations, I am . . .
_____
_____

How will I make today great?
_____
_____

DATE __/__/20__

Do what you can, with what you have, where you are.
—Theodore Roosevelt

I am grateful for
1. _____
2. _____
3. _____

I admire/appreciate/am proud of myself
1. _____
2. _____
3. _____

I learnt today/yesterday
1. _____
2. _____

Made me feel truly ALIVE,
☐ Meditation/silence _____
☐ Exercise/yoga/dance _____
☐ Reading _____
☐ _____

Daily affirmations, I am . . .
_____
_____

How will I make today great?
_____
_____

DATE __/__/20__

Success is not final, failure is not fatal: it is the courage to continue that counts.
—Winston S. Churchill

I am grateful for
1. _____
2. _____
3. _____

I admire/appreciate/am proud of myself
1. _____
2. _____
3. _____

I learnt today/yesterday
1. _____
2. _____

Made me feel truly ALIVE,
☐ Meditation/silence _____
☐ Exercise/yoga/dance _____
☐ Reading _____
☐ _____

Daily affirmations, I am . . .
_____
_____

How will I make today great?
_____
_____

Forgiveness day!
List the actions and behaviour you need to forgive in yourself and in another.

DATE __/__/20__

And, when you want something, all the universe conspires in helping you to achieve it.
—Paulo Coelho

I am grateful for
1. _____
2. _____
3. _____

I admire/appreciate/am proud of myself
1. _____
2. _____
3. _____

I learnt today/yesterday
1. _____
2. _____

Made me feel truly ALIVE,
☐ Meditation/silence _____
☐ Exercise/yoga/dance _____
☐ Reading _____
☐ _____

Daily affirmations, I am . . .
_____
_____

How will I make today great?
_____
_____

DATE __/__/20__

*Happiness is not something ready made.
It comes from your own actions.*
—Dalai Lama XIV

I am grateful for

1. _____
2. _____
3. _____

I admire/appreciate/am proud of myself

1. _____
2. _____
3. _____

I learnt today/yesterday

1. _____
2. _____

Made me feel truly ALIVE,

☐ Meditation/silence _____
☐ Exercise/yoga/dance _____
☐ Reading _____
☐ _____

Daily affirmations, I am . . .

_____
_____

How will I make today great?

_____
_____

DATE __/__/20__

Many people are alive but don't touch the miracle of being alive.
—Thich Nhat Hanh

I am grateful for
1. _____
2. _____
3. _____

I admire/appreciate/am proud of myself
1. _____
2. _____
3. _____

I learnt today/yesterday
1. _____
2. _____

Made me feel truly ALIVE,
☐ Meditation/silence _____
☐ Exercise/yoga/dance _____
☐ Reading _____
☐ _____

Daily affirmations, I am . . .
_____
_____

How will I make today great?
_____
_____

DATE __/__/20__

*The quantum field responds not to what we want;
it responds to who we are being.*
—Joe Dispenza

I am grateful for
1. _____
2. _____
3. _____

I admire/appreciate/am proud of myself
1. _____
2. _____
3. _____

I learnt today/yesterday
1. _____
2. _____

Made me feel truly ALIVE,
☐ Meditation/silence _____
☐ Exercise/yoga/dance _____
☐ Reading _____
☐ _____

Daily affirmations, I am . . .
_____
_____

How will I make today great?
_____
_____

DATE __/__/20__

If you think something is missing in your life, it is probably you.
—Robert Holden

I am grateful for

1. _____
2. _____
3. _____

I admire/appreciate/am proud of myself

1. _____
2. _____
3. _____

I learnt today/yesterday

1. _____
2. _____

Made me feel truly ALIVE,

☐ Meditation/silence _____
☐ Exercise/yoga/dance _____
☐ Reading _____
☐ _____

Daily affirmations, I am . . .

_____
_____

How will I make today great?

_____
_____

DATE __/__/20__

*Generosity is giving more than you can,
and pride is taking less than you need.*
—Khalil Gibran

I am grateful for
1. _____
2. _____
3. _____

I admire/appreciate/am proud of myself
1. _____
2. _____
3. _____

I learnt today/yesterday
1. _____
2. _____

Made me feel truly ALIVE,
☐ Meditation/silence _____
☐ Exercise/yoga/dance _____
☐ Reading _____
☐ _____

Daily affirmations, I am . . .
_____
_____

How will I make today great?
_____
_____

There is no sense in punishing your future for the mistakes of your past. Forgive yourself, grow from it, and then let it go.
—Melanie Koulouris

<u>A love letter to myself</u>

_____

DATE __/__/20__

The relationship you have with yourself sets the tone for every other relationship you have.
—Jane Travis

I am grateful for
1. _____
2. _____
3. _____

I admire/appreciate/am proud of myself
1. _____
2. _____
3. _____

I learnt today/yesterday
1. _____
2. _____

Made me feel truly ALIVE,
☐ Meditation/silence _____
☐ Exercise/yoga/dance _____
☐ Reading _____
☐ _____

Daily affirmations, I am . . .
_____
_____

How will I make today great?
_____
_____

DATE __/__/20__

A memory without the emotional charge is called wisdom.
—Joe Dispenza

I am grateful for

1. _____
2. _____
3. _____

I admire/appreciate/am proud of myself

1. _____
2. _____
3. _____

I learnt today/yesterday

1. _____
2. _____

Made me feel truly ALIVE,

☐ Meditation/silence _____
☐ Exercise/yoga/dance _____
☐ Reading _____
☐ _____

Daily affirmations, I am . . .

_____
_____

How will I make today great?

_____
_____

DATE __/__/20__

Owning our story and loving ourselves through that process is the bravest thing that we'll ever do.
—Brene Brown

I am grateful for
1. _____
2. _____
3. _____

I admire/appreciate/am proud of myself
1. _____
2. _____
3. _____

I learnt today/yesterday
1. _____
2. _____

Made me feel truly ALIVE,
☐ Meditation/silence _____
☐ Exercise/yoga/dance _____
☐ Reading _____
☐ _____

Daily affirmations, I am . . .
_____
_____

How will I make today great?
_____
_____

DATE __/__/20__

We can control our lives by controling our perceptions.
—Bruce H. Lipton

I am grateful for
1. _____
2. _____
3. _____

I admire/appreciate/am proud of myself
1. _____
2. _____
3. _____

I learnt today/yesterday
1. _____
2. _____

Made me feel truly ALIVE,
☐ Meditation/silence _____
☐ Exercise/yoga/dance _____
☐ Reading _____
☐ _____

Daily affirmations, I am . . .
_____
_____

How will I make today great?
_____
_____

DATE __/__/20__

Enlightenment is understanding that there is nowhere to go, nothing to do, and nobody you have to be except exactly who you're being right now.
—Neale Donald Walsch

I am grateful for

1. _____
2. _____
3. _____

I admire/appreciate/am proud of myself

1. _____
2. _____
3. _____

I learnt today/yesterday

1. _____
2. _____

Made me feel truly ALIVE,

☐ Meditation/silence _____
☐ Exercise/yoga/dance _____
☐ Reading _____
☐ _____

Daily affirmations, I am . . .

_____
_____

How will I make today great?

_____
_____

DATE __/__/20__

You yourself, as much as anybody in the entire universe, deserve your love and affection.
—Buddha

I am grateful for
1. _____
2. _____
3. _____

I admire/appreciate/am proud of myself
1. _____
2. _____
3. _____

I learnt today/yesterday
1. _____
2. _____

Made me feel truly ALIVE,
☐ Meditation/silence _____
☐ Exercise/yoga/dance _____
☐ Reading _____
☐ _____

Daily affirmations, I am . . .
_____
_____

How will I make today great?
_____
_____

Forgiveness day!
List the actions and behaviour you need to forgive in yourself and in another.

DATE __/__/20__

Discipline creates lifestyle.
—Hal Elrod

I am grateful for
1. _____
2. _____
3. _____

I admire/appreciate/am proud of myself
1. _____
2. _____
3. _____

I learnt today/yesterday
1. _____
2. _____

Made me feel truly ALIVE,
☐ Meditation/silence _____
☐ Exercise/yoga/dance _____
☐ Reading _____
☐ _____

Daily affirmations, I am . . .
_____
_____

How will I make today great?
_____
_____

DATE __/__/20__

Hate the sin, love the sinner.
—Mahatma Gandhi

I am grateful for
1. _____
2. _____
3. _____

I admire/appreciate/am proud of myself
1. _____
2. _____
3. _____

I learnt today/yesterday
1. _____
2. _____

Made me feel truly ALIVE,
☐ Meditation/silence _____
☐ Exercise/yoga/dance _____
☐ Reading _____
☐ _____

Daily affirmations, I am . . .
_____
_____

How will I make today great?
_____
_____

DATE __/__/20__

Put yourself at the top of your to-do list every single day and the rest will fall into place.
—Anonymous

I am grateful for
1. _____
2. _____
3. _____

I admire/appreciate/am proud of myself
1. _____
2. _____
3. _____

I learnt today/yesterday
1. _____
2. _____

Made me feel truly ALIVE,
☐ Meditation/silence _____
☐ Exercise/yoga/dance _____
☐ Reading _____
☐ _____

Daily affirmations, I am . . .
_____
_____

How will I make today great?
_____
_____

DATE __/__/20__

If you want a new outcome, you will have to break the habit of being yourself, and reinvent a new self.
—Joe Dispenza

I am grateful for
1. _____
2. _____
3. _____

I admire/appreciate/am proud of myself
1. _____
2. _____
3. _____

I learnt today/yesterday
1. _____
2. _____

Made me feel truly ALIVE,
☐ Meditation/silence _____
☐ Exercise/yoga/dance _____
☐ Reading _____
☐ _____

Daily affirmations, I am . . .
_____
_____

How will I make today great?
_____
_____

DATE __/__/20__

You have to believe in yourself when no one else does—that makes you a winner right here.
—Venus Williams

I am grateful for
1. _____
2. _____
3. _____

I admire/appreciate/am proud of myself
1. _____
2. _____
3. _____

I learnt today/yesterday
1. _____
2. _____

Made me feel truly ALIVE,
☐ Meditation/silence _____
☐ Exercise/yoga/dance _____
☐ Reading _____
☐ _____

Daily affirmations, I am . . .
_____
_____

How will I make today great?
_____
_____

DATE __/__/20__

The real difficulty is to overcome how you think about yourself.
—Maya Angelou

I am grateful for

1. _____
2. _____
3. _____

I admire/appreciate/am proud of myself

1. _____
2. _____
3. _____

I learnt today/yesterday

1. _____
2. _____

Made me feel truly ALIVE,

☐ Meditation/silence _____
☐ Exercise/yoga/dance _____
☐ Reading _____
☐ _____

Daily affirmations, I am . . .

_____
_____

How will I make today great?

_____
_____

Acknowledging the good that is already in your life is the foundation for all abundance.
—Eckhart Tolle

<u>A love letter to myself</u>

DATE __/__/20__

The relationship you have with yourself sets the tone for every other relationship you have.
—Jane Travis

I am grateful for
1. _____
2. _____
3. _____

I admire/appreciate/am proud of myself
1. _____
2. _____
3. _____

I learnt today/yesterday
1. _____
2. _____

Made me feel truly ALIVE,
☐ Meditation/silence _____
☐ Exercise/yoga/dance _____
☐ Reading _____
☐ _____

Daily affirmations, I am . . .
_____
_____

How will I make today great?
_____
_____

DATE __/__/20__

Your thoughts are incredibly powerful. Choose yours wisely.
—Joe Dispenza

I am grateful for
1. _____
2. _____
3. _____

I admire/appreciate/am proud of myself
1. _____
2. _____
3. _____

I learnt today/yesterday
1. _____
2. _____

Made me feel truly ALIVE,
- [ ] Meditation/silence _____
- [ ] Exercise/yoga/dance _____
- [ ] Reading _____
- [ ] _____

Daily affirmations, I am . . .
_____
_____

How will I make today great?
_____
_____

DATE __/__/20__

Love is the great miracle cure. Loving ourselves works miracles in our lives.
—Louise Hay

I am grateful for
1. _____
2. _____
3. _____

I admire/appreciate/am proud of myself
1. _____
2. _____
3. _____

I learnt today/yesterday
1. _____
2. _____

Made me feel truly ALIVE,
☐ Meditation/silence _____
☐ Exercise/yoga/dance _____
☐ Reading _____
☐ _____

Daily affirmations, I am . . .
_____
_____

How will I make today great?
_____
_____

DATE __/__/20__

If you don't love yourself, nobody will. Not only that, you won't be good at loving anyone else. Loving starts with the self.
—Wayne Dyer

I am grateful for
1. _____
2. _____
3. _____

I admire/appreciate/am proud of myself
1. _____
2. _____
3. _____

I learnt today/yesterday
1. _____
2. _____

Made me feel truly ALIVE,
☐ Meditation/silence _____
☐ Exercise/yoga/dance _____
☐ Reading _____
☐ _____

Daily affirmations, I am . . .
_____
_____

How will I make today great?
_____
_____

DATE __/__/20__

*Never give up on anyone.
And that includes not giving up on yourself.*
—Dieter Uchtdorf

I am grateful for
1. _____
2. _____
3. _____

I admire/appreciate/am proud of myself
1. _____
2. _____
3. _____

I learnt today/yesterday
1. _____
2. _____

Made me feel truly ALIVE,
☐ Meditation/silence _____
☐ Exercise/yoga/dance _____
☐ Reading _____
☐ _____

Daily affirmations, I am . . .
_____
_____

How will I make today great?
_____
_____

DATE __/__/20__

Inner peace begins the moment you choose not to allow another person or event to control your emotions.
—Pema Chodron

I am grateful for
1. _____
2. _____
3. _____

I admire/appreciate/am proud of myself
1. _____
2. _____
3. _____

I learnt today/yesterday
1. _____
2. _____

Made me feel truly ALIVE,
☐ Meditation/silence _____
☐ Exercise/yoga/dance _____
☐ Reading _____
☐ _____

Daily affirmations, I am . . .
_____
_____

How will I make today great?
_____
_____

DATE __/__/20__

Conscious thoughts, repeated often enough, become unconscious thinking.
—Joe Dispenza

I am grateful for
1. _____
2. _____
3. _____

I admire/appreciate/am proud of myself
1. _____
2. _____
3. _____

I learnt today/yesterday
1. _____
2. _____

Made me feel truly ALIVE,
☐ Meditation/silence _____
☐ Exercise/yoga/dance _____
☐ Reading _____
☐ _____

Daily affirmations, I am . . .
_____
_____

How will I make today great?
_____
_____

Forgiveness day!
List the actions and behaviour you need to forgive in yourself and in another.

DATE __/__/20__

Your perspective is always limited by how much you know. Expand your knowledge and you will transform your mind.
—Bruce Lipton

I am grateful for
1. _____
2. _____
3. _____

I admire/appreciate/am proud of myself
1. _____
2. _____
3. _____

I learnt today/yesterday
1. _____
2. _____

Made me feel truly ALIVE,
☐ Meditation/silence _____
☐ Exercise/yoga/dance _____
☐ Reading _____
☐ _____

Daily affirmations, I am . . .
_____
_____

How will I make today great?
_____
_____

DATE __/__/20__

The most creative act you will ever undertake is the act of creating yourself.
—Deepak Chopra

I am grateful for
1. _____
2. _____
3. _____

I admire/appreciate/am proud of myself
1. _____
2. _____
3. _____

I learnt today/yesterday
1. _____
2. _____

Made me feel truly ALIVE,
☐ Meditation/silence _____
☐ Exercise/yoga/dance _____
☐ Reading _____
☐ _____

Daily affirmations, I am . . .
_____
_____

How will I make today great?
_____
_____

DATE __/__/20__

The future depends on what we do in the present.
—Mahatma Gandhi

I am grateful for
1. _____
2. _____
3. _____

I admire/appreciate/am proud of myself
1. _____
2. _____
3. _____

I learnt today/yesterday
1. _____
2. _____

Made me feel truly ALIVE,
☐ Meditation/silence _____
☐ Exercise/yoga/dance _____
☐ Reading _____
☐ _____

Daily affirmations, I am . . .
_____
_____

How will I make today great?
_____
_____

DATE __/__/20__

The quantum field responds not to what we want; it responds to who we are being.
—Joe Dispenza

I am grateful for

1. _____
2. _____
3. _____

I admire/appreciate/am proud of myself

1. _____
2. _____
3. _____

I learnt today/yesterday

1. _____
2. _____

Made me feel truly ALIVE,

☐ Meditation/silence _____
☐ Exercise/yoga/dance _____
☐ Reading _____
☐ _____

Daily affirmations, I am . . .

_____
_____

How will I make today great?

_____
_____

DATE __/__/20__

Silence is the language of god, all else is poor translation.
—Rumi

I am grateful for
1. _____
2. _____
3. _____

I admire/appreciate/am proud of myself
1. _____
2. _____
3. _____

I learnt today/yesterday
1. _____
2. _____

Made me feel truly ALIVE,
☐ Meditation/silence _____
☐ Exercise/yoga/dance _____
☐ Reading _____
☐ _____

Daily affirmations, I am . . .
_____
_____

How will I make today great?
_____
_____

DATE __/__/20__

If you carry joy in your heart, you can heal any moment.
—Neale Donald Walsch

I am grateful for

1. _____
2. _____
3. _____

I admire/appreciate/am proud of myself

1. _____
2. _____
3. _____

I learnt today/yesterday

1. _____
2. _____

Made me feel truly ALIVE,

☐ Meditation/silence _____
☐ Exercise/yoga/dance _____
☐ Reading _____
☐ _____

Daily affirmations, I am . . .

_____
_____

How will I make today great?

_____
_____

We are all here for some special reason. Stop being a prisoner of your past. Become the architect of your future.
—Robin Sharma

<u>A love letter to myself</u>

DATE __/__/20__

Love cannot be explained, yet it explains all.
—Elif Shafak

I am grateful for
1. _____
2. _____
3. _____

I admire/appreciate/am proud of myself
1. _____
2. _____
3. _____

I learnt today/yesterday
1. _____
2. _____

Made me feel truly ALIVE,
☐ Meditation/silence _____
☐ Exercise/yoga/dance _____
☐ Reading _____
☐ _____

Daily affirmations, I am . . .
_____
_____

How will I make today great?
_____
_____

DATE __/__/20__

If you focus on the known, you get the known. If you focus on the unknown, you create a possibility.
—Joe Dispenza

I am grateful for
1. _____
2. _____
3. _____

I admire/appreciate/am proud of myself
1. _____
2. _____
3. _____

I learnt today/yesterday
1. _____
2. _____

Made me feel truly ALIVE,
☐ Meditation/silence _____
☐ Exercise/yoga/dance _____
☐ Reading _____
☐ _____

Daily affirmations, I am . . .
_____
_____

How will I make today great?
_____
_____

DATE __/__/20__

Gratitude is one of the most medicinal emotions we can feel. It elevates our moods and fills us with joy.
—Sara Avant Stover

I am grateful for
1. _____
2. _____
3. _____

I admire/appreciate/am proud of myself
1. _____
2. _____
3. _____

I learnt today/yesterday
1. _____
2. _____

Made me feel truly ALIVE,
☐ Meditation/silence _____
☐ Exercise/yoga/dance _____
☐ Reading _____
☐ _____

Daily affirmations, I am . . .
_____
_____

How will I make today great?
_____
_____

DATE __/__/20__

Our task is not to seek for love, but merely to seek and find all the barriers within yourself that you have built against it.
—Rumi

I am grateful for
1. _____
2. _____
3. _____

I admire/appreciate/am proud of myself
1. _____
2. _____
3. _____

I learnt today/yesterday
1. _____
2. _____

Made me feel truly ALIVE,
☐ Meditation/silence _____
☐ Exercise/yoga/dance _____
☐ Reading _____
☐ _____

Daily affirmations, I am . . .
_____
_____

How will I make today great?
_____
_____

DATE __/__/20__

The thing about meditation is that you become more you.
—David Lynch

I am grateful for
1. _____
2. _____
3. _____

I admire/appreciate/am proud of myself
1. _____
2. _____
3. _____

I learnt today/yesterday
1. _____
2. _____

Made me feel truly ALIVE,
☐ Meditation/silence _____
☐ Exercise/yoga/dance _____
☐ Reading _____
☐ _____

Daily affirmations, I am . . .
_____
_____

How will I make today great?
_____
_____

DATE __/__/20__

Meditation makes the entire nervous system go into a field of coherence.
—Deepak Chopra

I am grateful for
1. _____
2. _____
3. _____

I admire/appreciate/am proud of myself
1. _____
2. _____
3. _____

I learnt today/yesterday
1. _____
2. _____

Made me feel truly ALIVE,
☐ Meditation/silence _____
☐ Exercise/yoga/dance _____
☐ Reading _____
☐ _____

Daily affirmations, I am . . .
_____
_____

How will I make today great?
_____
_____

Forgiveness day!
List the actions and behaviour you need to forgive in yourself and in another.

_____
_____
_____
_____
_____
_____
_____
_____
_____
_____
_____
_____
_____
_____
_____
_____
_____
_____
_____
_____
_____
_____
_____
_____
_____
_____

DATE __/__/20__

> We can't create a new future while we're living in our past.
> It's simply impossible.
> —Joe Dispenza

I am grateful for

1. _____
2. _____
3. _____

I admire/appreciate/am proud of myself

1. _____
2. _____
3. _____

I learnt today/yesterday

1. _____
2. _____

Made me feel truly ALIVE,

☐ Meditation/silence _____
☐ Exercise/yoga/dance _____
☐ Reading _____
☐ _____

Daily affirmations, I am . . .

_____
_____

How will I make today great?

_____
_____

DATE __/__/20__

Skills are cheap, passion is priceless.
—Gary Vaynerchuk

I am grateful for
1. _____
2. _____
3. _____

I admire/appreciate/am proud of myself
1. _____
2. _____
3. _____

I learnt today/yesterday
1. _____
2. _____

Made me feel truly ALIVE,
☐ Meditation/silence _____
☐ Exercise/yoga/dance _____
☐ Reading _____
☐ _____

Daily affirmations, I am . . .
_____
_____

How will I make today great?
_____
_____

DATE __/__/20__

Anything that is of value in life only multiplies when it is given.
—Deepak Chopra

I am grateful for

1. _____
2. _____
3. _____

I admire/appreciate/am proud of myself

1. _____
2. _____
3. _____

I learnt today/yesterday

1. _____
2. _____

Made me feel truly ALIVE,

☐ Meditation/silence _____
☐ Exercise/yoga/dance _____
☐ Reading _____
☐ _____

Daily affirmations, I am . . .

_____
_____

How will I make today great?

_____
_____

DATE __/__/20__

You know why it's hard to be happy—it's because we refuse to LET GO of the things that make us sad.
—Bruce Lipton

I am grateful for
1. _____
2. _____
3. _____

I admire/appreciate/am proud of myself
1. _____
2. _____
3. _____

I learnt today/yesterday
1. _____
2. _____

Made me feel truly ALIVE,
☐ Meditation/silence _____
☐ Exercise/yoga/dance _____
☐ Reading _____
☐ _____

Daily affirmations, I am . . .
_____
_____

How will I make today great?
_____
_____

DATE __/__/20__

You cannot be lonely if you like the person you are alone with.
—Wayne Dyer

I am grateful for
1. _____
2. _____
3. _____

I admire/appreciate/am proud of myself
1. _____
2. _____
3. _____

I learnt today/yesterday
1. _____
2. _____

Made me feel truly ALIVE,
☐ Meditation/silence _____
☐ Exercise/yoga/dance _____
☐ Reading _____
☐ _____

Daily affirmations, I am . . .
_____
_____

How will I make today great?
_____
_____

DATE __/__/20__

Your "I CAN" is more important than your IQ.
—Robin Sharma

I am grateful for
1. _____
2. _____
3. _____

I admire/appreciate/am proud of myself
1. _____
2. _____
3. _____

I learnt today/yesterday
1. _____
2. _____

Made me feel truly ALIVE,
☐ Meditation/silence _____
☐ Exercise/yoga/dance _____
☐ Reading _____
☐ _____

Daily affirmations, I am . . .
_____
_____

How will I make today great?
_____
_____

*If you love life, do not waste time.
Because time is what life is made of.*
—Bruce Lee

<u>A love letter to myself</u>

DATE __/__/20__

*The best lesson I have learned in life came from
the worst feeling I ever felt in life.*
—Jay Shetty

I am grateful for

1. _____
2. _____
3. _____

I admire/appreciate/am proud of myself

1. _____
2. _____
3. _____

I learnt today/yesterday

1. _____
2. _____

Made me feel truly ALIVE,

☐ Meditation/silence _____
☐ Exercise/yoga/dance _____
☐ Reading _____
☐ _____

Daily affirmations, I am . . .

_____
_____

How will I make today great?

_____
_____

DATE __/__/20__

Our beliefs control our bodies, our minds, and thus our lives...
—Bruce Lipton

I am grateful for
1. _____
2. _____
3. _____

I admire/appreciate/am proud of myself
1. _____
2. _____
3. _____

I learnt today/yesterday
1. _____
2. _____

Made me feel truly ALIVE,
☐ Meditation/silence _____
☐ Exercise/yoga/dance _____
☐ Reading _____
☐ _____

Daily affirmations, I am . . .
_____
_____

How will I make today great?
_____
_____

DATE __/__/20__

*You've got to wake up every morning with determination
if you're going to go to bed with satisfaction.*
—George Lorimer

I am grateful for
1. _____
2. _____
3. _____

I admire/appreciate/am proud of myself
1. _____
2. _____
3. _____

I learnt today/yesterday
1. _____
2. _____

Made me feel truly ALIVE,
☐ Meditation/silence _____
☐ Exercise/yoga/dance _____
☐ Reading _____
☐ _____

Daily affirmations, I am . . .
_____
_____

How will I make today great?
_____
_____

DATE __/__/20__

*Never regret your past. Rather,
embrace it as the teacher that it is.*
—Robin Sharma

I am grateful for
1. _____
2. _____
3. _____

I admire/appreciate/am proud of myself
1. _____
2. _____
3. _____

I learnt today/yesterday
1. _____
2. _____

Made me feel truly ALIVE,
☐ Meditation/silence _____
☐ Exercise/yoga/dance _____
☐ Reading _____
☐ _____

Daily affirmations, I am . . .
_____
_____

How will I make today great?
_____
_____

DATE __/__/20__

*If you are irritated by every rub,
how will your mirror be polished?*
—Rumi

I am grateful for
1. _____
2. _____
3. _____

I admire/appreciate/am proud of myself
1. _____
2. _____
3. _____

I learnt today/yesterday
1. _____
2. _____

Made me feel truly ALIVE,
☐ Meditation/silence _____
☐ Exercise/yoga/dance _____
☐ Reading _____
☐ _____

Daily affirmations, I am . . .
_____
_____

How will I make today great?
_____
_____

DATE __/__/20__

The character of our life is based upon how we perceive it.
—Bruce Lipton

I am grateful for

1. _____
2. _____
3. _____

I admire/appreciate/am proud of myself

1. _____
2. _____
3. _____

I learnt today/yesterday

1. _____
2. _____

Made me feel truly ALIVE,

☐ Meditation/silence _____
☐ Exercise/yoga/dance _____
☐ Reading _____
☐ _____

Daily affirmations, I am . . .

_____
_____

How will I make today great?

_____
_____

Forgiveness day!
List the actions and behaviour you need to forgive in yourself and in another.

_____
_____
_____
_____
_____
_____
_____
_____
_____
_____
_____
_____
_____
_____
_____
_____
_____
_____
_____
_____
_____
_____
_____
_____
_____

DATE __/__/20__

Remind yourself that you cannot fail at being yourself.
—Wayne Dyer

I am grateful for

1. _____
2. _____
3. _____

I admire/appreciate/am proud of myself

1. _____
2. _____
3. _____

I learnt today/yesterday

1. _____
2. _____

Made me feel truly ALIVE,

☐ Meditation/silence _____
☐ Exercise/yoga/dance _____
☐ Reading _____
☐ _____

Daily affirmations, I am . . .

_____
_____

How will I make today great?

_____
_____

DATE __/__/20__

*Reading is to the mind what exercise is to the
body and prayer is to the soul.
We become the books we read.*
—Hal Elrod

I am grateful for
1. _____
2. _____
3. _____

I admire/appreciate/am proud of myself
1. _____
2. _____
3. _____

I learnt today/yesterday
1. _____
2. _____

Made me feel truly ALIVE,
☐ Meditation/silence _____
☐ Exercise/yoga/dance _____
☐ Reading _____
☐ _____

Daily affirmations, I am . . .
_____
_____

How will I make today great?
_____
_____

DATE __/__/20__

*Your soul will never be fully nourished by
anyone's love but your own.*
—Dominee

I am grateful for
1. _____
2. _____
3. _____

I admire/appreciate/am proud of myself
1. _____
2. _____
3. _____

I learnt today/yesterday
1. _____
2. _____

Made me feel truly ALIVE,
☐ Meditation/silence _____
☐ Exercise/yoga/dance _____
☐ Reading _____
☐ _____

Daily affirmations, I am . . .
_____
_____

How will I make today great?
_____
_____

DATE __/__/20__

*Others see their possibility in the reality of you.
Your message is your life lived.*
—Neale Donald Walsch

I am grateful for
1. _____
2. _____
3. _____

I admire/appreciate/am proud of myself
1. _____
2. _____
3. _____

I learnt today/yesterday
1. _____
2. _____

Made me feel truly ALIVE,
☐ Meditation/silence _____
☐ Exercise/yoga/dance _____
☐ Reading _____
☐ _____

Daily affirmations, I am . . .
_____
_____

How will I make today great?
_____
_____

DATE __/__/20__

No one is you and that is your power.
—Dave Grohl

I am grateful for
1. _____
2. _____
3. _____

I admire/appreciate/am proud of myself
1. _____
2. _____
3. _____

I learnt today/yesterday
1. _____
2. _____

Made me feel truly ALIVE,
☐ Meditation/silence _____
☐ Exercise/yoga/dance _____
☐ Reading _____
☐ _____

Daily affirmations, I am . . .
_____
_____

How will I make today great?
_____
_____

DATE __/__/20__

We are not human beings having a spiritual experience, but are spiritual beings having a human experience.
—Robin Sharma

I am grateful for
1. _____
2. _____
3. _____

I admire/appreciate/am proud of myself
1. _____
2. _____
3. _____

I learnt today/yesterday
1. _____
2. _____

Made me feel truly ALIVE,
☐ Meditation/silence _____
☐ Exercise/yoga/dance _____
☐ Reading _____
☐ _____

Daily affirmations, I am . . .
_____
_____

How will I make today great?
_____
_____

Swap "Why is this happening to me?" to "What is this trying to teach me?" It will change everything.
—Jay Shetty

<u>A love letter to myself</u>

DATE __/__/20__

When you do things from your soul,
you feel a river moving in you, a joy.
—Rumi

I am grateful for
1. _____
2. _____
3. _____

I admire/appreciate/am proud of myself
1. _____
2. _____
3. _____

I learnt today/yesterday
1. _____
2. _____

Made me feel truly ALIVE,
☐ Meditation/silence _____
☐ Exercise/yoga/dance _____
☐ Reading _____
☐ _____

Daily affirmations, I am . . .
_____
_____

How will I make today great?
_____
_____

DATE __/__/20__

How you do anything is how you do everything.
—Hal Elrod

I am grateful for
1. _____
2. _____
3. _____

I admire/appreciate/am proud of myself
1. _____
2. _____
3. _____

I learnt today/yesterday
1. _____
2. _____

Made me feel truly ALIVE,
☐ Meditation/silence _____
☐ Exercise/yoga/dance _____
☐ Reading _____
☐ _____

Daily affirmations, I am . . .
_____
_____

How will I make today great?
_____
_____

DATE __/__/20__

In order to love who you are, you cannot hate the experiences that shaped you.
—Andrea Dykstra

I am grateful for
1. _____
2. _____
3. _____

I admire/appreciate/am proud of myself
1. _____
2. _____
3. _____

I learnt today/yesterday
1. _____
2. _____

Made me feel truly ALIVE,
☐ Meditation/silence _____
☐ Exercise/yoga/dance _____
☐ Reading _____
☐ _____

Daily affirmations, I am . . .
_____
_____

How will I make today great?
_____
_____

DATE __/__/20__

*It's not who you are that holds you back,
it's who you think you're not.*
—Anonymous

I am grateful for
1. _____
2. _____
3. _____

I admire/appreciate/am proud of myself
1. _____
2. _____
3. _____

I learnt today/yesterday
1. _____
2. _____

Made me feel truly ALIVE,
☐ Meditation/silence _____
☐ Exercise/yoga/dance _____
☐ Reading _____
☐ _____

Daily affirmations, I am . . .
_____
_____

How will I make today great?
_____
_____

DATE __/__/20__

Nobody can hurt me without my permission.
—Mahatma Gandhi

I am grateful for
1. _____
2. _____
3. _____

I admire/appreciate/am proud of myself
1. _____
2. _____
3. _____

I learnt today/yesterday
1. _____
2. _____

Made me feel truly ALIVE,
☐ Meditation/silence _____
☐ Exercise/yoga/dance _____
☐ Reading _____
☐ _____

Daily affirmations, I am . . .
_____
_____

How will I make today great?
_____
_____

DATE __/__/20__

Glorify who you are today, do not condemn who you were yesterday, and dream of who you can be tomorrow.
—Neale Donald Walsch

I am grateful for
1. _____
2. _____
3. _____

I admire/appreciate/am proud of myself
1. _____
2. _____
3. _____

I learnt today/yesterday
1. _____
2. _____

Made me feel truly ALIVE,
☐ Meditation/silence _____
☐ Exercise/yoga/dance _____
☐ Reading _____
☐ _____

Daily affirmations, I am . . .
_____
_____

How will I make today great?
_____
_____

Forgiveness day!
List the actions and behaviour you need to
forgive in yourself and in another.

_____
_____
_____
_____
_____
_____
_____
_____
_____
_____
_____
_____
_____
_____
_____
_____
_____
_____
_____
_____
_____
_____
_____
_____
_____
_____
_____

DATE __/__/20__

*Dare to love yourself as if you were a
rainbow with gold at both ends.*
—Aberjhani

I am grateful for
1. _____
2. _____
3. _____

I admire/appreciate/am proud of myself
1. _____
2. _____
3. _____

I learnt today/yesterday
1. _____
2. _____

Made me feel truly ALIVE,
☐ Meditation/silence _____
☐ Exercise/yoga/dance _____
☐ Reading _____
☐ _____

Daily affirmations, I am . . .
_____
_____

How will I make today great?
_____
_____

DATE __/__/20__

How you love yourself is how you teach others to love you.
—Rupi Kaur

I am grateful for
1. _____
2. _____
3. _____

I admire/appreciate/am proud of myself
1. _____
2. _____
3. _____

I learnt today/yesterday
1. _____
2. _____

Made me feel truly ALIVE,
☐ Meditation/silence _____
☐ Exercise/yoga/dance _____
☐ Reading _____
☐ _____

Daily affirmations, I am . . .
_____
_____

How will I make today great?
_____
_____

DATE __/__/20__

If you have the ability to love, love yourself first.
—Charles Bukowski

I am grateful for

1. _____
2. _____
3. _____

I admire/appreciate/am proud of myself

1. _____
2. _____
3. _____

I learnt today/yesterday

1. _____
2. _____

Made me feel truly ALIVE,

☐ Meditation/silence _____
☐ Exercise/yoga/dance _____
☐ Reading _____
☐ _____

Daily affirmations, I am . . .

_____
_____

How will I make today great?

_____
_____

DATE __/__/20__

Your time is way too valuable to be wasting on people that can't accept who you are.
—Turcois Ominek

I am grateful for
1. _____
2. _____
3. _____

I admire/appreciate/am proud of myself
1. _____
2. _____
3. _____

I learnt today/yesterday
1. _____
2. _____

Made me feel truly ALIVE,
☐ Meditation/silence _____
☐ Exercise/yoga/dance _____
☐ Reading _____
☐ _____

Daily affirmations, I am . . .
_____
_____

How will I make today great?
_____
_____

DATE __/__/20__

To love oneself is the beginning of a life-long romance.
—Oscar Wilde

I am grateful for

1. _____
2. _____
3. _____

I admire/appreciate/am proud of myself

1. _____
2. _____
3. _____

I learnt today/yesterday

1. _____
2. _____

Made me feel truly ALIVE,

☐ Meditation/silence _____
☐ Exercise/yoga/dance _____
☐ Reading _____
☐ _____

Daily affirmations, I am . . .

_____
_____

How will I make today great?

_____
_____

Congratulations, you have completed 90 days of journaling.
Please celebrate it!

The more you praise and celebrate your life,
the more there is in life to celebrate.

Oprah Winfrey

Celebrate You.
Love,
Meher

You have known yourself a little more now, so who are you?

www.mehermirchandani.com

MEHER ANAND MIRCHANDANI is a maven who balances her various roles with equal ease and persistent hard work—whether it is that of a business leader, decision maker, wife, daughter, or a devoted mother to her twin daughters.

She leverages over fifteen years of rich experience as an entrepreneur in the fashion industry. As a cofounder of the iconic fashion brand Meher & Riddhima, she is acclaimed for having set benchmarks for other fashion brands in the UAE.

An award-winning entrepreneur, healer, and coach, Meher is the Director of Manrre Logistics Fund and Managing Director of Palmon Group. An inherently empathetic leader, she is a source of inspiration for her core team of leaders and leads by focusing on conscious leadership based on her personal and her company's values. As one of the *Forbes* top Indian leaders, Meher believes that culture is the cornerstone of an organisation, and she is responsible for creating and building a culture with a growth mindset at Palmon and Manrre that empowers leaders to build strong, motivated, and efficient teams.

Her leadership principle is "Success is something you attract by the person you become. It is your dedication to consistently grow yourself that will yield you the life you desire."

Her personal journey has brought about a breakthrough and transformation in her, which she shares in her first book.

Her mission is to evoke the transformation in you so you honour and celebrate yourself for who you are.

Meher can be contacted at: meher@mehermirchandani.com

To live is to give!

My purpose is to alleviate the pain in fellow humans so they are able to live a little easier. I aspire to do this in two ways—through my coaching and via contributions. I pledge to contribute the entire proceeds from the sales of my book, Come Alive and from my coaching fees to two foundations that are very close to my heart and resonate deeply with my values—Harmony House, India and the Palmon Foundation. Both these organisations focus on the betterment of lives, especially those of women and children via education and support. I believe education gives the ability to think with reason, pursue our dreams and aspirations, and live a worthy life in society.

Harmony House's key objectives are to provide a safe, fun, educational, and loving environment for children and women living in slums so they are able to perform respectable jobs and improve their standard of living.

Palmon Foundation provides scholarship to students in India, who aspire to pursue higher education. The programme runs diligently and caters to all aspects of achieving success for each student.

To know more about both these organisations and follow their work please visit Harmony House and Palmon Foundation Come join me on my mission www.mehermirchandani.com to empower you and contribute to a greater tomorrow.

I am grateful to you,

Love,

Meher Anand Mirchandani

www.ingramcontent.com/pod-product-compliance
Lightning Source LLC
Chambersburg PA
CBHW021022110526
R18276100001B/R182761PG44588CBX00009B/15